The Bestest Summer Ever

Brian Greytak

Dedication

For Rea Morris, who stuck by and believed in me.

And for "Bobo" Ifeanyichukwu Henry Onyeka~~BoBo~~ who made me believe that I could actually write a coherent sentence.

Acknowledgment

The author would like to thank the following for any and all support and friendship.

Todd Everts, Marcus and Analisa, Dave Andrews, Barry O'Rorke, Phil Whelan, and the entire HK theatre community.

CONTENTS

About the Author

Brian Greytak grew up in a small New England town where he first learned his love for baseball. As he became older, his interests expanded to the arts. This is his first stab at REAL writing. He hopes you enjoy reading it as much as he enjoyed bringing it to fruition.

Page Blank Intentionally

Chapter - 1

As he sat in the rocker on the porch of his typical Midwest home in Corn Husk, Nebraska, he wondered how it came to this. When had life decided to turn left when he went right? Coming to no conclusion, he sat back in his rocker, relit his pipe and went back to his crossword puzzle.

Then...

"Husband, hurry and get ready. They'll be here any minute."

"I've been ready since 7, wife. I showered, shaved and got dressed. How much more ready can I get?"

"Stop being stubborn and hurry," his wife said.

He slowly rose from his rocker, feeling the same twinges from arthritis he'd had for years.

Muttering under his breath as he went inside, "Not my idea of a good time taking care of some kid all summer."

"Stop muttering and get in here," she said in a more icy tone.

As he walked into the bedroom. He knew he would find a freshly pressed and clean set of clothes for this special occasion. Looking at the bed, his expectations had been met.

With a shrug, he changed his clothes and tried to remember what time Vanna was on.

Walking into the kitchen, he smelled the familiar aroma of chocolate chip cookies.

He reached for the plate of cookies on the counter and was rewarded with a slap on the wrist and a scowl from his wife, "Those are for Frankie!"

Just then, a car could be heard coming up the driveway with the seldom-heard crunch of gravel. They hadn't had many visitors since Elaine ran off right after graduating from the regional high school.

By the time he reached the front door, the kid was already out of the car, running like the wind to greet his grandma. Following slowly behind laden with two suitcases the size of boxcars, was Elaine. Frankie's mother and his daughter.

"Grandma! I've missed you so much," he said as he nestled into her welcoming arms.

"My, how you've grown! I don't think I can carry you on my hip anymore."

"Nope. I'm a big kid now. Hello, grandpa," he said and went in for a great big hug but was only rewarded with a firm handshake.

"Hiya, kiddo. Corn's getting high, ain't it?" his grandpa said.

Puzzled, Frankie turned to look at the cornfield that went on forever and a day. For a kid of ten, being from the city, that was a bunch of corn.

"Holy moly," he said. "Where does it end?"

Elaine finally made it up to the porch, out of breath and dripping sweat.

"Mom. So, so great to see you. You haven't aged a day since, well, you know."

Elaine's husband, Frankie Sr., died suddenly, five years earlier, from a heart attack. Leaving behind a young mother and 5-year-old son. How long has it been since I've come back, she thought? Just as well, this town reeks of decay and desolation.

Hugging her mother seemed to wake the memories that had haunted her for too many years.

"Oh honey, you look great!" her mother said. "Come inside and have a bite to eat. You must be famished from the long drive."

"Long drive!" her father said. "Hell, it's barely 2 hours as the crow flies."

Elaine looked at her father with a hatred borne of hidden secrets and memories best left forgotten.

"Hello, Father," she said and walked straight past him into the house. "Hey Frankie, I think I smell grandma's famous chocolate chip cookies."

"Oh boy! Can I have some mom?"

"Just a couple honey. Don't want to spoil your appetite for the feast I'm sure your grandma's fixed for lunch."

"Ok, Mom," he said as he raced around the house, trying to find the kitchen.

"Where's the kitchen?" he yelled. "This place is like a palace compared to our apartment."

"Just follow your nose," his grandma yelled back.

Her smile spoke volumes. Her baby was home. If only for a short while.

"Well, husband, I thought you wanted some cookies?"

"I lost my appetite. I think I'll just sit out here and smoke my pipe."

Shaking her head, she rushed into the house not wanting to waste one second with her daughter leaving right after lunch. He could just eat sour apples for all she cared and smiled at the thought of him doing just that.

He could tell lunch was about over. He heard dishes being washed and could catch a word or two of the conversation. Not that he cared that much. He hadn't cared for years. He'd been a good provider. Never complained much. The one big argument they had; he said some things that were best left unsaid. So, what if she overheard them? She was bound to find out sooner or later.

With that last thought, he nodded his head as if in agreement with himself, relit his pipe and started a new crossword puzzle.

A short time later Elaine burst through the screen door on her way to God knows where to do who knows what, he thought. She'd always had a mind of her own and was stubborn as a mule, just like her mother. There was love between them once, but that had disappeared just like she did after graduating high school. Only a short note to say goodbye to her mother and not to worry too much. Not a word for him. I guess I deserved that one, he thought.

Goodbyes and hugs were exchanged at the car, and the wife and kid watched her leave until there was nothing left to watch but the corn swaying in the hot summer breeze. He used to love this time of year. The smell of the crops in the field was always a favorite with Elaine. But now, he didn't even remember how to love. He felt hollow inside and had no one to blame but himself.

The first ten years or so were pretty darn good. Lots of laughs. Watching Elaine grow up was easy on the eyes. She and Frankie Jr. are peas in a pod. He looks just like his mother at that age. Full of questions and boundless energy. He could never keep up with her.

One day, while playing hide and seek with Elaine, he hid so well that she couldn't find him.

"Okay, Dad, I give up," she said.

Except, he didn't answer. They found him an hour later, collapsed behind the old Victrola in the shed. He was rushed to the hospital, where he was diagnosed with a heart attack. They found he had a faulty aortic valve. Been there all his life, they said. Surgery to fix it was successful, but his energy never seemed to get back to normal.

He was a changed man after that. Kept to himself mostly. No more hide and seek for him. No siree, Bob. That kid almost killed me once, he thought. He continued working at the factory, as usual, but his heart and head wouldn't let him rest from the trauma caused by that darn kid.

He retired ten years later with a decent pension. After 36 years of hard work, his bum ticker, as he would call it, finally called it a day and forced his early retirement.

With nothing to do all day, he turned to crossword puzzles and game shows on TV. Not much of a life but at least he owned his house free and clear. He still drove the old 65' Chevy wagon he bought brand new. Only 25k on the odometer. I think I'll be buried in it, he thought. Let her walk everywhere when I'm gone. Serve her right.

He found the letters the day before their fifth anniversary. That was the first and only time he drank alcohol. He wound up at the local beer joint a few towns over. Never made it home that night or the next night either. Slept in the back of the wagon. He doesn't remember much of those two days, but he sure remembers the hangover.

"Never again will I touch a drop," he said out loud to no one in particular.

But he heard himself loud and clear. Ain't touched so much as the bottle the wife has hidden under the kitchen sink. Another secret he wished he never knew.

He never had a problem with other people drinking. In fact, his Pops used to make his own hooch. Made a good living at it until some hillbilly hick got jealous and ratted him out. Pops spent 5 years in prison, too far away to visit back then. We never knew when he was released. In fact, never heard from him again. Mom was heartbroken and drank herself to death not long after his release. That's why he never drank until that God-awful night.

The letters! All that sappy love shit between the two of them. Sickening. Why did she hide so much from me? What else could she be hiding? Did she ever really love me? I guess I went a bit too far that night. Said some things I regret, he thought. What did she expect, though? I got feelings, too, dammit. By then, the smoke from his pipe looked like a locomotive chugging along the rickety old train tracks behind the old Grange Hall. He noticed this and put the pipe down. Smoking too much, he thought. Or so the doctor says.

He stood up and headed back inside. The sound of one of those ridiculous cartoons was turned up way too loud.

"Shoot, the kid already took over the TV. Almost time for Price is Right, too."

He sat down in his recliner and reached for the TV to change the channel when his wife said, "Don't you dare touch that TV. Frankie's our grandson and deserves to enjoy his vacation with us."

"Ayah, grandson!" he said and retreated to the porch and his rocker. "Looks like you and I are going to be great pals this summer," he said to the rocker.

From inside, the wife yelled, "You've been great pals since you found that piece of junk when you disappeared for two days."

"It ain't a piece of junk. It's a Bassett rocker made in Virginia. None finer. Now keep quiet, wife, and turn that TV down. They can hear it all the way to Hogs Holler."

Hogs Holler was just a little spit of a town. One dirt road going straight through, end to end. Too much inbreeding in that slop pile, he thought. Supposedly, they make the best hooch in five counties. The feds have been after that place for years. Never could find the stills. They may be inbred, but they sure know how to fool the feds. He chuckled at that last bit. He had no use for the feds since his Pops got caught making the best hooch in Nebraska. It was the inbred folks from Hogs Holler that ratted Pops out. I bet my life on it.

"What's Hogs Holler, Grandpa?" the kid asked. He hadn't heard the kid come out to the porch.

"Didn't see you there, kid," he said. "It's just a little slop pile of a town with a bunch of inbreds."

"What's a slop pile?" Frankie asked.

"Just a pile of trash we feed the hogs," Grandpa said.

"Can I help next time you feed the hogs?"

"We ain't got no hogs kiddo. Just a lot of crows making a racket every day around sunset. Oh, and one rooster ain't cockadoodledooed in two years."

"What's a cockado?"

"Too many questions kiddo. Go see if you can help your grandma. Skeeters will eatcha alive out here. Don't want your mom any madder at me than she is."

"Why is Mom mad at you?"

"WIFE," he hollered so loud that the crows began an early chorus of their Sunset Serenade, "Give the kid something to do."

"I'm busy, husband. Dinner doesn't make itself."

"Tastes like it sometimes," he muttered.

"I heard that!" she said louder and sharper than usual. "It's your turn to entertain Frankie."

The finality of the statement left him no choice.

"Hey, kiddo," he said. "Why don't you go and look at the stuff in your mother's room?"

"Gee, can I?"

"No reason why you can't. Just don't make a mess."

"OK, thanks, Grandpa."

"Don't mention it, kiddo. Have fun!"

As much fun as you can have looking through smelly, old junk, he thought.

Chapter - 2

Frankie searched for his mother's room. It's not that the house was a palace; he just didn't know his way around yet.

Behind the first door was what looked like a laundry room. It had a couple of machines that looked ominous in the shadows. He quickly shut the door and continued down the hall. The next door he opened, he knew it had to be his mother's room. There were posters of bands and people he never heard of. The walls were painted in various neon colors. He was hesitant about looking through his mom's stuff without her permission, but curiosity gave him a hard shove that almost made him fall flat on his face. He looked behind him as if to complain, but there was no one there.

He contemplated turning the lights on, but the sun still had plenty before going to sleep. The room had four windows. Two each facing south and west. The bed was big enough to sleep a family of four, he thought. On each side of the bed, there were nightstands painted neon green. On the left, there was a lamp, with some kind of shawl thrown over it, a notebook and an ashtray. I didn't know mom smoked, he thought. On the right nightstand, he saw the strangest thing. It was about fifteen inches tall, with some clear yellowish liquid at the top and opaque red liquid at the bottom. Not sure of what it was, he looked all around it and found an electrical cord attached to it running to the wall socket, with an off-and-on switch near the base.

Being as curious as ten-year-olds can be, he flipped the switch, and a light shone up from the bottom.

"That's it?" he said out loud.

He didn't know what to expect, but he thought it would be more interesting.

He left the light on and continued his search for any hidden treasure he might find. In this room, he felt like a famous archeologist inspecting the ruins of a lost civilization. He knew it was silly, but it was so unlike the rest of the house that it felt ancient.

His first step was to just look but touch nothing else. The lamp was such a disappointment that he decided to choose his next excavation site carefully. Suddenly, he noticed a movement from on his left. He jumped and nearly tripped over some long-forgotten pair of sneakers. When he looked again, he saw that the movement came from inside the lamp. Strange, he thought, as the red liquid was moving up toward the top of the lamp in different shapes. He didn't know what this thing was but, he knew he must find out.

Again, he looked closely at the lamp. He touched it, and it was warm. Almost too warm to touch very long. But he decided to pick it up, just for a few seconds. He checked the bottom and found a sticker. In big red letters, it read "LAVA LAMP". Now, he knew volcanoes made lava, but he couldn't figure out how they could get it into a lamp. He'd ask Grandpa later. He gently put the lamp back. Still staring at it, he was amazed at the shapes it continued to make. He never, in his life, imagined hot lava could be put into a lamp.

He wasn't sure what to explore next. The chest of drawers looked inviting, but he thought it best to ask his mother first before going through the drawers. Now, the closet to the right was fair game, though. He opened the door and saw a string hanging down from the ceiling. Pulling the string, he was rewarded with a treasure trove of artifacts. He was beginning to like this archeology stuff. Stepping into the closet, he could hear the call of the strange things he saw.

The floor was littered with shoes that looked like nothing he had ever seen. There was every color of the rainbow represented. There were shoes with heels and soles that could make someone as tall as Andre the Giant. That was his favorite WWF wrestler. He watched every WWF program he could.

He soon lost interest in the shoes. Hanging all around him were the clothes of some lost civilization. Colors and patterns he never imagined. He dared to touch one. It was smooth to the touch, yet when he pulled on it, it stretched easily. He continued down the line of clothes. Touching each one as if it were gold. Toward the back of the closet, his foot bumped against something solid. Looking down, he saw a big square box with a gold clasp on it. He knew he shouldn't open it, but he couldn't resist.

Looking back over his shoulder to make sure no one was watching, he slowly bent down to examine the clasp. He pushed a small button, and the clasp popped open with a loud snap. He fell back on his rear end, feeling as if he had been pushed.

It's not locked, he thought. That means it must be ok to look inside. He didn't know why but his hands were trembling as he reached to open the box. He took a deep breath and held it in. The lid opened with no trouble. Slowly, he raised the lid. Inside, he found a plethora of books, magazines, records, and so much more.

He picked up a pile of magazines with titles like Teen Beat, People, and others. Most he didn't recognize. Laying the pile aside, he picked up another. Underneath this pile, there was a box that said Prince Albert Tobacco. Strange, he thought; I guess mom really did smoke.

He gently took the box out and put it on his lap. Slowly and carefully, he raised the lid. In it were some very strange things indeed. He picked up a ring with a black stone in it. He put it on and raised his hand toward the light to get a better look. He noticed the stone was changing colors to a bright blue. He immediately took it off and watched as the stone turned black again. Now, this was a real find. It must be some sort of ancient magic.

Next, he picked up what looked like a small pipe. The bowl was the size of a walnut with some sort of screen in the bottom. He brought it up to his nose and sniffed. Yuck, he thought. He had never smelled tobacco like that before. Putting down the pipe, he reached for a glass tube that looked like something from a laboratory. Yet, it was different. It was open on one end with a small hole halfway down the tube. There was also a metal tube sticking out of another hole. Attached to the tube was what looked like a bowl the size of a cherry pit. This one had no screen in it. What was this thing, and why would Mom hide it, he thought?

He promised himself to ask Grandpa about this later. He continued to rummage around in the box. Pushing stacks of records aside, he noticed yet another small box. This must be pretty valuable if mom took the time to hide it so well.

In his excitement, he dropped the box, and the contents spilled out. There wasn't much inside. Only a few postcards, a seashell necklace, and an earring. He picked up the postcards and started looking through them. The first had a picture of Old Faithful and Yosemite Park. On the next card, there was a picture of the Space Needle from the 1962 World's Fair. He could tell there was only one more postcard, but it was stuck to the back of the second one.

He examined it more closely and ever so gently began to pry the two cards apart. It took him what seemed like ages, but it was only a few seconds. Staring at the last card he could only see what looked like a smaller card wrapped in tissue paper and sealed with tape so old it had yellowed and lost most of its sticky stuff.

At once, he knew this must be very important to his mother. He delicately unwrapped it and found that it was only a baseball card. He didn't recognize the player and he knew every player on every team. He started his baseball card collection when he was five, right after his father died. Thinking about his father didn't make him cry anymore. He could hardly remember his face.

He blinked his eyes and shook his head as if to wake from a trance. Looking down, he noticed that he had dropped the card. Picking it up, he began to examine it more closely. The front had a picture of what looked like a young man holding a bat. The name read Pernell "Slinky" Whitiker. What a strange name he had. He turned the card over and looked at the back, where he knew the lifetime stats of the player were listed. Reading them, he could see that he was a very good player. He led the league in stolen bases three years in a row. His lifetime batting average was just above 300. Why would his mother save this card and hide it so well?

Just then, he could hear his grandmother setting the table for dinner.

He began to put everything back in place when he heard his grandpa yell, "Hey, kiddo, get cleaned up. Time for dinner."

He looked one last time at the card and came to a decision. I think I'll keep this and ask Grandpa about it, he thought, when he didn't know. But soon.

His grandmother made potato pancakes and kielbasa with sauerkraut for dinner. His mother must have told her it was his favorite.

His grandfather raised his bushy white eyebrows and said, "What's the occasion? You ain't made this in years."

"This is Frankie's favorite," she replied. "Used to be Elaine's too, remember?"

"So it was," was all he had to say on that matter. Looking at Frankie, he said, "Whats the matter, kiddo, not hungry? Dig in! Your grandma made this just for you."

Frankie needed no more encouragement. He forked three pancakes at once. Piled sauerkraut on each and took the biggest piece of kielbasa just as his grandpa was reaching for it. He was about to say something to the kid, but his wife threw daggers his way and shook her head slightly. He knew when he was beating a dead horse. Don't think I can take 2 months of this shit, he thought.

The conversation at dinner was all one-sided. Frankie talked non-stop between mouthfuls. My teacher said this, my mom told me, blah blah blah was all heard until his ears picked up a smidgen of talk from his wife.

"What did you get up to before dinner?" she asked.

"Oh, not much. Grandpa said I could look at the stuff in mom's room."

"Did he now?" she said while giving her husband a look that could stop clocks. He never raised his head and kept right on eating.

"Find anything interesting?" she asked.

"Did you know that they can take hot lava and put it in a lamp?" he asked in all seriousness.

"Where did you hear that, dear?" his grandma asked.

"I didn't hear, I saw it."

"Is that so?" Grandpa growled, knowing full well where the kid saw it.

"Yep! My mom has a lamp in her room that has a sticker on the bottom. It said, "LAVA LAMP", just as plain as day."

"My, my! The things they come up with nowadays," Grandma said.

Having polished off eight pancakes with the biggest piece of kielbasa and half the sauerkraut, Frankie announced, "That was the bestest ever Grandma!"

Gathering up the dishes, she leaned over, kissed Frankie on the forehead, and, with a sigh, said, "Your mother used to say the same thing, sweetie. You're so much like her."

"HMPFF," was all husband could manage to say. He rose from the table and announced that he would be on the porch watching the corn grow.

'Kiddo, help your grandma with the dishes."

"Yes, sir!" he said with a salute and a big smile.

Not amused, his grandpa said, "There'll be no more of that in this house," and he stormed to the porch, slamming the screen door behind him. "That kid is more like his mother than I thought."

Frankie was about to ask his grandma what he did wrong, but she just shook her head and said, "Not now, dear."

With that said, he cleared the table and helped with the dishes.

The next few days went pretty much the same. Frankie was restless but was trying to be patient. The baseball card was neatly tucked in his shirt pocket, waiting for the right time for its revealing.

That night, Frankie was sitting on the porch with his grandpa, watching the corn grow. There seem to be more cars on the road tonight, he thought.

"Hey Grandpa."

"What's up, kiddo?"

"Where are all the cars going tonight?"

"I'm guessing they're heading to the park down the road," Grandpa said.

"There's a park close by?" Frankie asked.

"Yep. Just a spit away."

"I can't spit very far. Besides, my mom says spitting isn't nice."

"Well, your mom is right. Spitting ain't what a gentleman does."

"That makes you a gentleman then. I've never seen you spit."

Grandpa had to chuckle at that one and said, "You might be right. Grandma might have other thoughts on the subject, though."

"So, Grandpa, what's going on at the park tonight?"

"I reckon it's the first home game of the season for the Corn Huskers."

"Baseball!" Frankie said with a look of awe on his face.

"You like baseball kiddo?"

"Sure do. I'm the starting shortstop for my school team."

"Shortstop, you say! Doesn't surprise me in the least."

"Why's that grandpa?"

"Makes no, never mind, kiddo."

"Okay," Frankie replied. "Can I show you something, Grandpa?"

"Sure, kiddo. Whatcha got?"

Frankie handed him the baseball card he found in his mom's closet.

A look of pure hatred spread across his grandpa's face, replaced quickly with a slight smirk.

"What's wrong, Grandpa?"

"Not a thing, kiddo. Where abouts did you come across this?"

"Am I in trouble, Grandpa?"

"No, kiddo. I'm just surprised to see it, that's all."

"Who is it, and why would Mom save it?"

"He's just some two-bit player that ruined everything he touched."

"But his stats show that he was pretty good.'

"Life ain't all about baseball stats, kiddo," Grandpa mused.

"Would you take me to a game sometime, please, Grandpa?" Frankie begged.

"Don't like baseball. You can go if you want, though. The park ain't far at all."

"Really!? Tonight?" Frankie asked in amazement.

"Maybe tomorrow, kiddo. Let's see how it goes."

Disappointed, Frankie hung his head and said, "Whatever you say, Grandpa."

But he just knew he had to see the Corn Huskers play. *I never imagined there would be a real professional baseball team way out here,* he thought.

Chapter - 3

Frankie waited a few days, hoping his grandpa would mention going to watch the Corn Huskers. He just couldn't wait any longer. So, that night at dinner, he mentioned it to his grandparents.

"When can I go to see the Corn Huskers play?"

"Maybe your grandpa will take you some time. He used to go all the time," she said.

"He told me he doesn't like baseball," Frankie whined.

"He did, did he?" she said while scowling at her husband.

"Maybe he could go by himself. It's right down the road some," Grandpa growled.

Nodding her head, Grandma said, "I suppose that would be alright."

"Wowee. When?"

A shrug from his grandpa was all Frankie got in reply.

"Hey, grandma," Frankie said as he pulled out the baseball card from his shirt pocket. "Why did mom save this card?"

Taking the card, she studied it carefully. Then, a small grin on her face and twinkle in her eye told Frankie that somehow his grandma knew but wouldn't say.

"Maybe you should ask your mother about it."

With a grunt, his grandpa stood up from the table so fast that his chair fell to the floor with a loud bang. He stared at his wife for a good ten seconds, then turned and walked out to the porch.

"Have fun with your old friend, Mr. Rocker," his wife said with a touch of sarcasm.

"Is Grandpa okay?" Frankie asked.

"I doubt it," she replied. "Don't worry, dear; it's not your fault. Now, how about some lemon meringue pie for dessert?"

"Sure!" Frankie forgot all about baseball for the time being and dove into the pie like a pig into slop.

The next night, after dinner, Grandpa and Frankie were again sitting on the porch watching the corn grow when Frankie felt a slight tap on the back of his head. He turned around to look and saw his grandpa holding a five-dollar bill.

"Thought you might like to walk down and see a game tonight. I hear that two-bit player is the manager of the Huskers."

Frankie took the money and just stared at his grandpa.

"What are you waiting for?" Grandpa said. "The game starts at 6:30. Only about a ten-minute walk from here. Down the driveway, take a right and walk until you see the park. Lights ain't on yet, but you can't miss it."

With money in hand, Frankie turned and started running down the driveway.

"Hey, kiddo." Frankie stopped and turned back to look at his grandpa. "Be careful walking there, and be sure to get a hot dog and some popcorn. Seems I recall they used to be some pretty dagum good eatin'."

"I will, Grandpa. Thanks so much. Love you!" On that note, Frankie turned and ran like the wind. He didn't want to miss one pitch. After all, this was his first professional baseball game.

His grandpa watched until Frankie disappeared around the bend and nodded as if to say, 'That's settled'. As he lit his pipe, he couldn't help but smile at the wonderment of youth.

He remembered many a night spent at that park. Eating hot dogs until he was about to burst. In fact, it was on just one of those nights that he saw the most beautiful girl he'd ever seen. He made up his mind then and there that he would marry that girl someday. Of course, he never mentioned it to any of his friends there with him that night. He knew they would give him a hard time.

He made an excuse of needing to use the bathroom and made his way over to the girl. She was busy chatting with one of the players, so he busied himself with the game until the Corn Huskers took the field.

Waking from his memories, he lit his pipe and wondered why life was so cruel sometimes. Shaking his head, he went inside to watch Wheel of Fortune. There's always Vanna's ass, he thought and grinned like a schoolboy.

Frankie was out of breath after his run to the park. Hands on his knees, he sucked in a couple of deep breaths. Looking up, he caught his first glimpse of the park. Wow! He thought. This is huge! Looking around, he noticed a few cars parked haphazardly around him. In his excitement, he ran right past them on his way in.

He finally caught sight of the entrance. Next to it was a small booth with a sign on the top that read, "TICKETS HERE". He made a beeline straight for the booth.

Money in hand, he asked the lady selling tickets, "One, please?"

"How old are you, son?" she asked.

"Just turned ten last month, ma'am," he replied.

"First time to a game?" she queried.

"Yes, ma'am, this is the first professional game in my life."

With a chuckle and a grin, she said, "First-timers are free of charge. Enjoy the game."

"Thank you very much," he replied. "Can I ask you a question?"

"Sure thing, kid. What is it?"

"I have this baseball card here." Reaching into his shirt pocket, he produced the card. "My grandpa says this guy is the manager of the Corn Huskers. Can I meet him?"

She took the card, and sure enough, it was indeed the manager.

"You'll find him on the first base side by the dugout. Not sure if you want to meet him though. He's grouchy and doesn't talk much. Especially to kids."

"Thanks," he said. "I'm sure he'll talk to me. I'm a big kid now. Maybe he'll even sign my card."

Shaking her head, she said, "Good luck with that."

Once inside the park, Frankie stood in awe. There were bleachers on both sides of the field, running way down to the warning track and stopping at the outfield fence. They were painted in many different colors, which had faded over the years. The outfield fence was painted green with ads for local businesses running from foul pole to foul pole. On top of the ads, next to the foul poles, were the distance markers from home plate. Each side read 320 feet in white. In dead center field, it read 400 feet. Four hundred feet, he thought, with his mouth hanging open.

It was then he smelled what could only be hot dogs on a grill. He scanned the park and saw a sign that read Snack Bar this way with a red arrow pointing to a building by the entrance. He finished dinner less than an hour ago, but he couldn't resist that pull of the hot dog calling his name.

Walking up to the snack bar, he looked up and saw the menu board. They sell more than hot dogs, he thought. There were burgers, fries, onion rings, corn dogs (whatever those are), he thought. They also had fried bologna sandwiches. They were the bestest; his mom made them all the time. He decided to order one of those with a Tab to drink.

When he got to the stands, he saw that maybe a hundred people had decided to attend the game. He decided on a seat on the first base side hoping to talk with the manager. Sitting down, he dove into his sandwich, hoping they were as good as his mother's. His expectations were met and exceeded. This is the bestest fried bologna sandwich ever, he thought.

Just then, the announcer introduced a local girl who would sing the national anthem. Everyone stood with their hands over their hearts and sang along. Just like on TV, Frankie thought. She's not very good, though. Frankie cringed when the girl tried to hit the high notes. Almost over, he thought.

The anthem finally finished; the starting lineups were read out. First the visiting team was presented to a spattering of applause.

"And now, presenting tonight's lineup for your very own Corn Huskers!" the announcer boomed.

Everyone stood and cheered for the home team.

The last person announced was the manager, Cap Whitiker. Cap? Frankie thought. Cap stepped out of the dugout, tipped his hat, and sat back down.

Play Ball! The Homeplate umpire yelled. With that, Frankie sat down to watch his first professional baseball game.

The pitcher threw a few warmup pitches. On the last pitch, the catcher threw the ball down to second base. The shortstop caught the ball and pretended to tag out a phantom runner. He then tossed it to the second baseman, who then threw it to the third baseman. On to the first baseman, who walked over to the pitcher, handed him the ball, slapped him on the backside and trotted back to his position.

By the time Frankie realized it, it was the fourth inning, and the lights were turned on, flooding the field and making it like daylight.

He still hadn't gotten up the nerve to talk to the manager. Maybe during the seventh-inning stretch, he thought.

Well, the stretch came and went without Frankie making a move to talk with the manager. He didn't know why he was so nervous, but he felt like this wasn't the right time to approach the manager. After all, he was in the middle of managing a game. Maybe after the game, I'll do it, he thought.

The game ended with the Huskers losing 5-1. That didn't matter much to Frankie. It was now or never.

"Excuse me, Mr. Whitiker," he shouted louder than he had intended.

"Yeah," Cap growled in reply.

"Can I speak to you, please?"

"Not now, kid," he said in reply.

As Cap turned around to see who the kid was, he was stopped in his tracks. This kid looks familiar, he thought. With that, he shook his head and walked into the clubhouse.

Dejected. Frankie turned and followed a group of people leaving the park. Once outside the park, Frankie saw his grandpa leaning against the ticket booth, smoking his pipe and chatting with the lady who sold tickets.

"Hey, Grandpa," he shouted.

He ran straight to his grandpa, gave him a big hug and said, "That was the bestest game ever. They had fried bologna sandwiches, so I bought one. They even let me in for free because it was my first game. They're playing tomorrow and……"

"Whoa, slow down, kiddo. Take a breath," Grandpa said with a grin. "Who let you in for free?" Grandpa asked.

"That old lady you were just talking to," Frankie said.

"That'd be Gladys. She always had a soft spot for the young'uns," Grandpa replied. "Although, I'm not sure if she would take to being called old."

"You know her?"

"Sure do, kiddo. She's been selling tickets for as long as I can remember."

"I thought you said you didn't like baseball, grandpa."

"Used to. Don't anymore," he replied.

"Why not? Baseball is the bestest!"

"Makes no, never mind," he said.

Then Grandpa thought back to the last time he went to a game. Had to be almost thirty years. Elaine used to love to come and watch the Huskers. Yeah, well, she used to love a lot of things. Then she didn't. His smile turned to a grimace. Almost as if he was in pain.

"What's wrong, grandpa? Are you okay?"

Coming back to the present, he nodded as if to say best, let sleeping dogs lie.

With a grunt, he pushed himself from the ticket booth and said, "Yeah, kiddo. Never better."

But that was about as true as saying the crows sang a happy tune each day at sunset.

On the way home, Frankie talked non-stop about each player, the crowd and how the manager wouldn't talk to him after the game.

"Doesn't surprise me. That feller drinks too much of that rock gut. He's always in a sour mood," Grandpa said. "Listen to that kiddo. Sounds like those darn crows are doing an encore performance tonight."

"It sure does, Grandpa."

As they turned into the driveway, Frankie thought about asking what rock gut was when he saw his grandma standing silhouetted by the light of the porch. Moths were doing a dance around her head as he raced to the porch, nearly knocking her over. She laughed and picked him up for a quick hug. Frankie wanted to tell her all about the game, but she insisted it was time for bed.

"Aw, grandma, Do I have to?" Frankie whined.

"Yes, dear. Now hurry on in before your bath water gets cold."

He shuffled his feet and replied sadly, "Yes, grandma. The fried bologna sandwich was the bestest though. Even better than moms."

He then ran into the house, leaving a trail of clothes behind him.

Fried bologna sandwiches, she thought. Elaine used to say the same thing. Those sandwiches at the park were always better than mine. She chuckled to herself and turned to go into the house when her husband walked right past her.

Talking as he walked through the door, "Elaine used to say those sandwiches were the bestest, too."

She couldn't be sure, but she thought his eyes glistened like he was about to cry. She decided to sit in his rocker made in Virginia and wait until he got comfortable in front of the TV.

She felt hot tears running down her cheeks and thought, if only he hadn't found those letters.

Chapter - 4

The next morning at breakfast, Grandpa was nowhere to be found, and Grandma looked like she had been crying all night. Frankie thought about asking what was wrong but decided to try and cheer her up instead.

"Hey, grandma," he said in his best happy voice. "Want to hear a dirty joke?"

She looked up as if just noticing he was there and said, "Sure, dear."

"The pig fell in the mud," he said.

She couldn't help but laugh, thinking that was Elaine's favorite 'Dirty Joke' too.

Noticing her smile, he decided to continue with another joke, "How about a clean joke Grandma?"

"Much better," she said with a tone only a grandmother could use. She knew what was coming next but couldn't resist hearing Frankie say it.

"The pig got washed off," he replied.

This time, his grandma grinned from ear to ear. Elaine used to tell the same jokes every time I was feeling down, she remembered. He certainly is just like his mother!

"Where's Grandpa?" he asked.

"He's not feeling well this morning, Frankie. He'll get up in time to watch Vanna on Wheel of Fortune." More like Vanna's ass, she thought.

"Maybe my jokes would make him feel better," he said.

"Not today, dear. Maybe another time."

"Okay," he said and proceeded to pick up his bowl of cereal and drain the remaining milk with a big slurp.

Yep, just like his mother, she thought. "Now go and brush your teeth and enjoy the morning. It's a beautiful day!"

With breakfast finished, Frankie did as he was told. After he was done brushing his teeth, Frankie went out to the front porch. He wanted to try out Grandpa's rocker. To his surprise, Grandpa was already rocking away and smoking his pipe.

"I didn't know you were here Grandpa. Are you feeling better now? Grandma said you weren't feeling well."

"Right as rain," he said. "Say, kiddo."

"Yes Grandpa."

"Why don't you run out to the mailbox and get this old man his morning newspaper?"

"Sure thing," he said. "Say, grandpa?"

"Hmmm," was his reply.

"That lady at the ticket booth is old. You ain't nowhere near as old as her."

"Thanks, kiddo. Now run down and get that paper."

The kid was beginning to grow on him.

Out of breath after running to get the paper, Frankie sat down on the porch and handed the paper to his grandpa when he suddenly remembered something.

"Hey, Grandpa, I almost forgot. Here's your change from last night."

"Keep it kiddo. They're playing again tonight. Say, how much money do you have left?"

Frankie took out some crumpled bills from his pocket and proceeded to count the money. Trying to flatten them out on the porch, he was satisfied that they were finally ready to be counted.

Grandpa watched him silently count the bills and all the coins. Frankie's tongue was sticking out the side of his mouth as he finished. He thought back to a time when Elaine sat right there doing the same thing the same way. He hadn't realized how much he missed the little things in life. I need to make some changes, he thought.

When Frankie looked up, Grandpa was smiling.

"There's four dollars and fifty cents left. Wow, food sure is cheap at the park," Frankie said in amazement.

"Hmmm," Grandpa said. "Might not be enough for today's game. It's a doubleheader. The first game starts at 3:30. Here, take this too." He handed him another five-dollar bill and slowly lit his pipe.

"Gee, thanks, grandpa. But I'll miss supper. Won't grandma be mad?"

"Don't worry, kiddo. I'll talk to her later. Let's keep our secret for now. Oh, and no talk about the money. Deal?"

"Deal," Frankie said with a big smile. He then walked up to his grandpa, climbed on his lap, and whispered in his ear, "Don't worry, I know how to keep a secret. You're the bestest grandpa ever. I love you."

At that moment, Grandma opened the screen door and said, "What are you two scoundrels whispering about."

"Nothing, Grandma. Grandpa was just going to show me how to do a crossword puzzle. Isn't that right, grandpa?"

"Righto, kiddo. Let's get started," he said and gave Frankie a wink as if to say good job, kiddo.

Little did they know, but Grandma had heard the whole conversation. Except what Frankie whispered in her husband's ear. Will wonders never cease, she thought. She hadn't seen her husband so happy since.......... best not think too much and enjoy the change Frankie was bringing about for all of them.

During lunch, Grandpa was true to his word, "Wife," he said. "Frankie is going to miss dinner tonight."

"My goodness, why on earth would he miss dinner?"

"There's a doubleheader today, and I told him it was alright to head to the park after lunch. Thought he could watch some batting practice."

With a scowl and a shake of her head, she said, "Whatever you think is best, husband." Gathering up the dishes she turned and walked back toward the sink.

She thought that things might be okay after all when Frankie said, "I think I'll help grandma with the dishes, Grandpa."

"Good idea, kiddo. Think I'll go and see what's on the boob tube," Grandpa said.

"What's a boob tube?" Frankie asked.

"TV, kiddo, TV," Grandpa turned and walked to the living room.

Elbows on the counter and chin in hands, Frankie watched his grandma wash the dishes. He looked deep in thought with a serious expression on his face.

"Why so serious, dear?"

"I've been trying to figure something out. Can I ask you a serious question?"

"Of course, dear."

"Why does grandpa call you wife, and you call him husband?" he asked.

"Because dear, that's what we are," she replied.

"I know that. But don't you have names?"

"Of course we do. Hasn't your mother ever told you our names?"

"Nope. Never," he said. "So, what are your names?"

"Well, mine is Marge, and Grandpa is Steve."

"Okay, I like those names. You still haven't said why you call each other husband and wife."

"I guess it's because grandpa wants it that way, I suppose," she said with a tone that said, now, no more questions.

"Then why does he call me kiddo? I mean, he knows my name, doesn't he?"

"What a silly question. Of course, he does."

"So, why then?"

"Maybe it's just his nickname for you. Why don't you ask him sometime."

"You don't think he'll get mad at me?"

"Goodness, no! Just ask him."

"Okay, thanks."

Now that Frankie got that off his chest, he grabbed a towel and began to dry the dishes.

His grandma watched him with a smile, but there was sadness in her eyes as she flashed back to that night when Elaine was the same age as Frankie. The things both she and her husband said needed to be said. But things got loud and out of hand. What Elaine heard, she never said. But after that night, things were never the same.

Grandpa heard every word of that conversation. She knows darn well why I do that, he thought. I have half a mind to set that kid straight. But then, he remembered that time twenty-five years ago when his wife and he had a big argument about the letters. Funny, he thought, I don't even think about her name anymore. Maybe it's time to let go of bad memories and try and get back to the way it used to be. Is that possible, he asked himself.

Deep in thought, he hadn't heard Frankie enter the living room. "Hey, Grandpa," he said.

With a startled look, he replied, "Sweet Jesus, kiddo. Make some noise when you enter a room. This bum ticker of mine can't take that kind of scarin'."

"Sorry, Grandpa. I really didn't mean to scare you. What's a bum ticker?"

"My heart kiddo."

"What's wrong with your heart, Grandpa?" Frankie asked while climbing on his lap. Giving him a big hug, he started to cry and asked, "You're not going to die, are you Grandpa?"

"Not yet, kiddo. Now, now, no need to cry. I still got things I need to set straight before I'm gone."

Grandpa sat there hugging Frankie as the tears rolled down his own face.

"Not yet, kiddo, not yet."

Taking out a handkerchief, Grandpa dried his own tears before wiping Frankie's cheeks.

He held it up to Frankie's nose and said, "Blow your nose, Frankie. We don't want Grandma to see two men crying. Do we?"

"No, sir." Frankie did as he was told, climbed down from his grandpa's lap, and said in a very serious tone, "We just became friends, I'm glad you're going to be okay."

"Nothing to worry about kid…er…. Frankie. Say, isn't it about time for you to get a move on? Don't want to miss batting practice."

"Oh boy, I almost forgot. Thanks, Grandpa. Will you pick me up after the games?"

"Sure, as the sun comes up every morning. I'll be waiting for you at the same place."

Frankie gave him another hug, kissed his cheek, and ran to the kitchen to do the same to his grandma.

With that settled, he charged out of the door and down the driveway like his pants were on fire.

Grandma watched Frankie run out of the house and sat down in one of the kitchen chairs. She had heard their conversation and wondered if this could be the best medicine for her husband's condition. Before Frankie arrived, he had been taking more of his medication than usual. Now, he seemed more at ease. I sure hope he meant what he said about setting things straight. It's been too many years already. Lord only knows how many we have left.

Taking out a tissue from her apron pocket, she wiped her eyes and blew her nose. This house has been too long without love was her final thought before rising and beginning to put the dried dishes back in the cabinet.

Chapter - 5

Frankie arrived at the park out of breath again.

Heading straight to the ticket booth, he said, "I'd like……one, please."

Gladys was manning the booth again and said, "Go right in, kid."

Frankie began to turn to leave but remembered he hadn't said thank you.

Turning back to Gladys, he said, "Thank you very much, ma'am. You're the bestest."

Taken aback, she muttered, "My pleasure." Where had she heard that word before? Been a long time. Twenty-five years or more, she thought. Then it hit her like a ton of bricks. Marge and Steve's kid used to say that. Could that be Elaine's kid?

"Hey, Gladys. Are you selling tickets today, or is everybody getting in free?"

She looked up and saw a line of people waiting to get into the park. "Keep your shirt on, Hank. Ain't as young as I used to be, ya know."

"Ain't that the truth. Still have a soft spot for the kids I see."

"Sometimes your mouth ain't good for nothing more than that awful rhubarb pie your mama used to make for every bake sale," she said with a smile.

"Twas pretty awful, gotta admit that. Even our dog, ole Duke, wouldn't eat it," Hank quipped.

That got a chuckle and a few words of agreement from the people in line.

"This ain't a hen party, Hank Malone. Get your tail feathers inside," Gladys shot back.

With a salute, he said, "Yes, ma'am," grabbed his ticket and off he went.

Frankie wasn't hungry yet, so he rushed to the same seat as yesterday. The visiting team was just finishing up batting practice. The Huskers hustled onto the field to start their pre-game routine. Most of them went to the outfield to stretch or do some wind sprints under the watchful eye of the manager. Cap Whitiker could be heard shouting to some of the players. He was calling some of them by some pretty strange names.

"You call that running Spanky?" he bellowed. "You ain't going now where fielding like that, Guppy," he said to another.

Frankie turned his attention to the batting cage, where a player swung and hit a weak dribbler down the third baseline.

"My mama could hit better than you, Slick, and she's been pushing up daisies near twenty years now," Cap hollered.

With the pre-game routine finished, the Huskers headed to the dugout. Once there, Frankie could hear Cap trying to give the team a pep talk. But the team was too busy yapping to hear him.

Cap bellowed, "Now listen up, you bunch of pancakes! Yesterday, you got beat by a team that's only got one guy who can play worth a spit."

The team quieted down and listened to another no-good pep talk from a no-good manager. Everyone knew that Cap carried a bottle of the cheapest hooch he could afford in his back pocket. In fact, he was probably already two sheets to the wind. It's going to be a long day, the players thought.

Cap continued, "Today, I'm mixing things up. Spanky! You're catching today and batting ninth. Slim, you're leading off today, and I don't want to see you swatting at flies out there. Keep your head down and swing through the pitch. The rest of you clowns can read the lineup posted behind me. Look out in those stands. Those folks didn't come to see you lose again. Try and look like you know what you're doing."

That being said, Cap took the bottle out of his back pocket and took a big swig. I should have bought that moonshine from that fella in Hogs Holler. He makes the best shine around these parts.

Lineups announced and the anthem sung, Frankie settled down to watch the game.

"Play ball," the umpire hollered. Frankie got goosebumps every time he heard those words.

"Baseball is the bestest," he said under his breath.

"Sure is, kid," the guy next to him said. "I've been coming to see the Huskers for right near forty years now. My pappy started bringing me here when I was younger than you."

"Wow," was all Frankie could manage as a reply.

His face was beet red. He hadn't realized that anyone heard him.

With the game tied 2-2 in the middle of the seventh inning, Frankie saw that the manager was standing right in front of him smoking a cigarette. It's now or never, he thought.

Gathering up his courage, he said in his most respectful voice, "Excuse me, Mr. Whitiker. Can I talk to you?"

"Middle of a game, kid," he growled.

Frankie sat down dejectedly when the guy next to him said, "Aw Cap, it's the seventh inning stretch. Give the kid a few minutes."

Crushing his cigarette under his cleat, he turned around to tell the guy just what he thought when he saw the same kid from yesterday. That kid looks like someone I know, he thought.

"Okay, okay, Jack. Just a couple of minutes. I got a game to manage."

"How about you manage to stay sober today, Cap," Jack shot back.

Glaring at Jack, he started to say something, but the words got caught in his throat. It's that kid, he thought. Gotta watch my language around him. He didn't know why, but he felt that he needed to be nice to this kid.

Looking at Frankie, he said, "What's on your mind, kid?"

Frankie's eyes gave away his excitement at being able to talk to a real -life baseball manager. At first, Frankie couldn't think of what to say. Then, he remembered the card in his pocket. In his excitement, he dropped the card on the grass next to Cap.

Cap picked up the card, looked at it and handed it back to him. Why does this kid have an old card of mine, he thought?

Just then, Frankie blurted out, "My grandpa says this is you."

Looking a bit confused, Cap replied, "That ain't me, kid. That guy had a couple of good years. I ain't done much but ruin everything I touch."

"Cap is right, kid," some player down in the dugout yelled.

Cap turned and yelled right back, "Slick, when you get your batting average higher than your age, you can say anything you want. Until then, shut your pie hole."

Frankie ignored their exchange and said, "Mr. Whitiker, would you sign my card, please?"

"Can't kid. It ain't me," he said as he walked down to the far end of the dugout.

Shaking his head, Frankie couldn't believe his grandpa was wrong. He made up his mind, then and there, to talk to Mr. Whitiker every chance he got.

The Huskers lost the first game 3-2 on an error in the eleventh inning. Cap was furious.

"All right you bush leaguers, into the clubhouse. If I see one smile when I get in there, I'll keep you here till midnight running drills."

He was standing right in front of Frankie, smoking another cigarette.

"My mom says that smoking is bad for you, Mr. Whitiker."

"Maybe so," he replied, turning around, "But these and hootch are the only things that matter to me, kid."

"I don't believe that," Frankie said. "Don't you have any family or friends?"

"Lost my only chance for a family too many years ago to remember," he said with a sadness in his voice that made Frankie more determined to make this man his friend.

"I can be your friend, Mr. Whitiker."

"No thanks, kid. I ain't nothing but a drunk. People don't hang around with guys like me."

"I will, sir," Frankie said with a determination that surprised him. "I'll come to every game just to talk with you."

"Sure you will, kid," and he slowly walked to the clubhouse.

True to his word, Frankie was sitting right there when the second game was about to start. He could see Cap down the other end of the dugout having a heated discussion with one of the players. He couldn't hear what was being said, but he knew that the player was the one who made the error that led to the loss in game one.

Cap walked back towards Frankie, deep in thought. "Hi, Mr. Whitiker. I bet that guy will concentrate more on the field now," he said.

Looking up in surprise, Cap said, "Hey, kid. He better, or he'll be shoveling coal back home."

"How long have you been a manager, Mr. Whitiker?"

"Can't rightly remember, kid. Longer than you've been alive, though."

"Wow! You must be a good manager then."

"Nah," Cap replied. "Nobody else wanted to come back out here and manage, so here I am."

"I'm glad you did," Frankie replied.

"You are?" Cap asked in disbelief. "Why's that?"

"Yes, sir. How else could we become friends?"

"Friends, huh? Been a long time since I had any friends," Cap replied with sadness in his voice.

"Don't worry, sir. I'll be your bestest friend."

"Thanks, kid. Time to get back to work."

"You're welcome. Can we talk more later?"

"We'll see, kid. Enjoy the game."

"You bet I will."

The seventh-inning stretch was there before Frankie realized. The Huskers were down 7-1. Cap was sitting in the dugout with a cigarette in one hand and a bottle of hootch in the other.

"Don't worry, sir," Frankie said. "I think you're going to win this game."

Cap was startled and almost dropped his bottle. "Geez, kid, give me some warning before you start gabbing to me."

"Sorry, sir."

"Ah, it's okay, kid. What makes you think we're gonna come back from six runs down?"

"Well, sir, the bottom of your lineup has been in a slump, but they've been swinging at good pitches. Just been hitting them in the wrong places."

"So, what's your solution to the problem kid?"

"You want my opinion, really?"

"I'll take anything at this point, kid."

"Well, you got number seven in the lineup leading off. He's fast enough to beat out a bunt. Once he's on first, I'd get him to steal second on the first pitch."

"Worth a try, kid. Why the first pitch, though?" Cap was beginning to think this kid might know more about baseball than some of his players.

"I noticed the pitcher has a real slow windup, and he hardly ever checks the baserunners," Frankie replied.

"Hmmm," was all Cap said.

Cap did, indeed, have the leadoff hitter bunt, and sure enough, he beat it out. I'll be a monkey's uncle. The kid was right, Cap thought.

On the next pitch, the runner took off for second base. He got such a huge jump on the pitch that the catcher didn't even attempt to throw him out.

"Well, kid, you were right. Thanks."

Frankie grinned from ear to ear. Imagine a big-league manager taking advice from me.

"Well, what do you say, kid? What next?"

In a hushed voice, Frankie said, "Have the runner steal third, and the batter lay down a bunt to the third base side."

Cap gave the signs, and again, it worked to perfection.

The number nine batter was up next, and again, Cap asked Frankie's strategy.

"Well, sir, they wouldn't expect another bunt," he said.

The batter laid down a perfect bunt that the pitcher had to field. His only play was to first base, except there was no one covering the bag. The runner scored from third. Men on first and second with no outs.

This strategy was just the motivation the team needed. They scored eight runs on seven hits. Cap looked at Frankie, winked, and nodded with a big smile.

The Huskers scored four more runs in the eighth on a grand slam that sailed over the 400-foot mark in dead center. It landed a good fifty feet into the cornfield.

The final score was 13-7 in favor of the Huskers. Could this be a sign that his team was coming alive, Cap thought. One could only hope.

Cap made a point of shaking Frankie's hand after the game. Frankie was so excited that he ran right past his grandpa, leaning against the ticket booth.

"Slow down, kiddo. Where's the fire?"

Frankie stopped in his tracks, turned around and ran straight to his grandpa and gave him a big hug.

"You won't believe what happened," he said.

"Is that right?" said. "Why don't you sleep on it tonight and we'll talk about it at breakfast."

"Sure, Grandpa, if you say so," Frankie said rather dejectedly.

"Grandma made something special for your snack before bedtime. Unless you filled up on fried bologna sandwiches that is."

"Oh boy! No sir, I only had one."

Grandpa chuckled, took Frankie's hand, and they walked home in the dark night. You could hear the corn rustling in the soft, warm summer breeze.

Life's not so bad, Grandpa thought.

Chapter - 6

The following day, the Huskers began an extended road trip that would last 2 weeks.

Sitting on the porch with his grandpa that evening, Frankie was pondering what to do for the next two weeks when his grandpa asked him, "Why so serious, kiddo?"

"No reason," he said. "Just wondering how the Huskers are making out."

"We can find out tomorrow when the paper gets here," Grandpa replied. "Why don't we take a walk in the cornfield and see if we can get the crows started a little early tonight?"

"Sure, Grandpa," Frankie said. "I've been wondering why those silly crows make such a racket every night."

"Good question, kiddo," was all Grandpa could say.

They walked in silence between the rows of corn when Frankie suddenly asked, "Is the corn really as high as an elephant's eye?"

"I see your mother has been educating you in the finer points of musical theater," he said with a chuckle.

"Well, in the movie Oklahoma, the guy said the corn was as high as an elephant's eye."

With a chuckle, his grandpa replied, "Your mother asked me the same thing many years ago."

With that said, Grandpa thought back to a night years before when he and Elaine walked the corn fields. She sure was an inquisitive one, he thought. Always wanting to know why things were the way they were. I never knew all the answers and just flew by the seat of my pants, he remembered fondly. She never doubted me. Putting his arm around Frankie's shoulder, he got a rather sad look on his face.

Looking up, Frankie noticed how sad his grandpa looked.

"Is something wrong, Grandpa," he asked.

"Not really, kiddo. Just remembering when times seemed much simpler."

"But why aren't things simple now?"

"Can I be honest with you, kiddo?" Grandpa asked in a very serious tone.

Stopping dead in his tracks, Frankie looked up lovingly at his grandpa and nodded.

Grandpa was quiet for a couple of minutes as he stood and watched a crow land on a cornstalk not five feet away. Nodding to himself as if to say, why not, he began to tell Frankie a story.

"You see, kiddo, your grandpa made some serious mistakes years ago. I said and did some things I'm not too proud of. The reasons don't seem to matter much anymore. Truth be told, I haven't talked to anyone about this, ever."

"Why, Grandpa?"

"Well, kiddo, I guess partly because I was ashamed and partly because I just never felt comfortable talking about it."

"I know how that feels," Frankie replied.

"Do tell," Grandpa said.

"Well, one time, and you can't tell my mom about this," Frankie said in all seriousness. "Promise?"

"Oh, I promise, alright. Just between us, men. The women need to never know," he said as he crossed his heart.

"Okay then," Frankie continued with his story. "One time, I was drinking some chocolate milk and spilled it all over Mom's favorite blanket on the couch. I told her that the cat jumped on my lap and knocked the glass out of my hand."

"What really happened?" Grandpa asked.

Sheepishly, Frankie said, "I just wasn't paying attention, and it slipped right out of my hand."

"Why didn't you just tell your mother the truth?

"I don't really know. I guess maybe I was scared. You're the only one I can tell."

"Do you feel better telling me? Do you think, maybe now, you can tell your mother the truth?"

"I do feel better after telling you. Not sure about telling mom, though."

"Well, best not to wait too long to tell her. Things tend to get more complicated the longer you wait."

"Is that what happened with you, Grandpa? Will you set things right, like you said?"

"That's exactly what happened, kiddo. The years just flew by. I'm waiting for the right time to set things right, though." Soon, he thought. "Skeeters are eating me alive, kiddo. Let's head back."

They turned around and walked back to the porch in a comfortable silence that made Grandpa even more determined to make things right again.

As they neared the porch, they saw Grandma sitting in the rocker made by Bassett, drinking a lemonade.

"Where have you two been," she asked.

"Just checking to see if the corn is as high as an elephant's eye," Grandpa said with a grin so big that his wife had to laugh out loud.

"And is it?" she asked.

"Seems to be," Frankie and Grandpa said at the same time.

They both looked at each other and couldn't hold back their laughter.

Smiling a smile, she didn't know she had in her anymore, she rose from the rocker and headed inside.

On the way inside, she said, "C'mon, you two. The snickerdoodles won't eat themselves."

With that, Frankie raced past his grandma on the way to the kitchen.

"Oh, wife," Grandpa said.

"Yes, husband."

Thinking this was as good a time as any to begin to set things right, he started to say, "I'm a…………"

"You're a what husband?"

Changing his mind, he said, "I'm in the mood for a glass of milk with those cookies. Would you mind if Frankie and I had them out here?"

Taken aback by his change in demeanor, she readily agreed and proceeded to bring out a tray with a pitcher of milk, three glasses and a pile of cookies to the porch with Frankie in tow.

"C'mon Frankie, let's the three of us have our snack out here. It's about time for those crows to start up."

In a flash, Frankie was out the door. That's odd, he thought; why is Grandpa sitting on the steps? His answer came when his grandpa said, "Marge, why don't you take the rocker tonight since you've been slaving over those cookies for hours."

"Thank you, Steve."

Just then, as if on cue, the crows began their sunset serenade, and the three of them laughed so hard and loud that even the crows had to stop and wonder where the racket was coming from. Only for a minute though, then they cranked it up a notch so as not to be outdone.

Chapter - 7

The next morning, Frankie was up early and running out the door before breakfast. Heading back into the house, newspaper in hand and out of breath from the run out to the mailbox, he neatly set the paper next to his grandpa's plate and took his seat at the table.

Preparing breakfast, his grandma said, "So that's what got you up so early. What's so important in the paper?"

His grandpa, walking into the kitchen, said, "We got to see how the Huskers did yesterday. Isn't that right, kiddo?"

"Yes, sir," Frankie said.

Grandpa picked up the paper and slowly scanned every page.

"Ah, there it is," he said. "What's a seven-letter word for………"

"Grandpa!" Frankie said with an air of exasperation. "C'mon."

With a smile and a chuckle, Grandpa read the byline in the sports section. "Huskers sweep the doubleheader. Move into third place."

"Wow, that's great," Frankie replied. "Keep going."

"Breakfast first, kiddo. Those pancakes won't eat themselves," Grandpa said as he smiled at his wife.

"That's right, Frankie. Don't let them get cold,' his grandma said.

So, Frankie dove into his pile of pancakes and wolfed them down quicker than you can say, flibbertigibbet.

"Finished already?" Grandpa asked.

"Yes, sir," he replied.

"Well then, why don't you take the paper out to the porch and read all about the games? Leave the crossword for me, though," he said with a wink at his wife. "Let me finish my coffee, and I'll join you. Then, you can give me the rundown."

"Thanks, Grandpa," he said and headed out to the porch.

When Grandpa looked up, his wife was looking at him like she had never seen him before.

"What's gotten into you," she asked.

"What do you mean?"

"Last night, you let me sit in your rocker, and today, you're acting strange."

"Nothing strange about being in a good mood," he said as he rose from his chair and put his dishes in the sink.

"There, when was the last time you helped clear the table?"

"Can't rightly remember, but I'll be doing more of it. You can be sure of that."

Walking out to the porch, he said, "Thanks for the delicious breakfast, Marge."

"My pleasure," she said.

Chapter - 8

The next few days passed in pretty much the same way. Grandpa and grandson are debating the finer points of the national pastime in the morning and watching game shows until Frankie's bedtime.

One beautiful Midwest morning with the dew still on the grass and corn, Grandpa asked Frankie, "Did you bring your glove with you?"

"Yes, sir," Frankie replied.

"Why don't you go out behind the shed and throw some balls against it to keep your arm strong? I even painted some circles on it so you can practice your accuracy, too."

"Gee, thanks, Grandpa," he said as he rushed inside to get his glove.

He made it back to the porch with the glove in hand as a look of sadness crossed his face.

"What's wrong, kiddo?"

"I didn't bring my ball," Frankie replied.

"I already thought of that," Grandpa said. "There's a bucket of balls waiting behind the shed for you."

"You're the bestest! Thanks, Grandpa," and off he went.

The wife overheard their conversation and decided to see how much her husband had changed.

Standing at the door, she said, "Why don't you go and play catch with him?"

"Why would I do that? Doc told me to take it easy," he said.

"It's a game of catch. You're not running a marathon."

"Bah, don't even have my glove anymore," he said.

"Is that right," she said.

"Right enough, wife. Anyway, my puzzle won't do itself."

"Hmpff," was her only reply.

The next morning at breakfast, Grandpa walked into the kitchen and, sitting where his plate should be, was his old Spaulding glove that he hadn't seen in years.

"Where did you find that?" he asked his wife.

"Oh, around," his wife replied.

Just then, Frankie appeared in the doorway to the kitchen.

"Hey, Grandpa, I didn't know you had a glove. Can we play catch sometime today?"

Seeing the twinkle in his wife's eye was all the encouragement he needed.

"Sure, kiddo. But you gotta take it easy on me. Been at least 25 years since I put this thing on."

"Don't worry, grandpa. I'm only ten and can't throw as hard as you."

"Why don't we find that out later kiddo?"

With that settled, the three of them ate kielbasa, eggs over easy and some hash brown potatoes.

"What a feast," Grandpa said. "What's the occasion?"

"It's your favorite, isn't it," his wife said matter of factly. "Oh, and here's your rye toast as well."

"That it is," Grandpa said with a smile and a nod. "Real nice of you, wife."

"It's my job," she said.

"It is? I guess maybe you need a raise then," he said with a chuckle.

True to his word, Grandpa and Frankie played catch that afternoon.

"We've been at it over two hours, kiddo. Let's give this old man a rest."

"Sure, Grandpa," Frankie said.

"Besides," Grandpa said, "I sure could use some of grandma's special lemonade. How about you?"

Before Frankie could answer, the screen door opened and out came Grandma with a pitcher of lemonade, three glasses and a piece of coconut cake for each of them.

"Amazing," Grandpa said. "My favorite cake too. You take the rocker wife. Frankie and I will sit on the steps and feed the ants while we eat with our hands."

"Now, husband, that's not how proper people eat," she said.

"Well, shoot. We don't feel much like being proper today. Do we kiddo?"

Frankie replied by picking up the biggest piece of cake in his hand and took a huge bite. With frosting on his nose, he looked down and did indeed see that the ants were enjoying the cake, too.

"Look, Grandpa, you were right. The ants like the cake, too."

"Sure enough, kiddo," Grandpa said with a hearty laugh.

When the cake was gone, Grandma said, "You two are a sight. Both of you run inside and clean up. It's about time for your show, husband. Wouldn't want to miss Vanna's ass."

Turning beet red, Grandpa did as he was told with Frankie close behind.

"Grandpa, why do you watch Vanna's ass," Frankie inquired.

At a loss for words, all Grandpa could manage was a cough and a mutter.

"I mean, doesn't grandma have an ass too?"

"Course she does kiddo. It's just that.........you'll understand when you get older."

"Mom says the same thing when she doesn't want to answer something."

"I expect she does," Grandpa said. "Now, go and turn on Wheel of Fortune and no more talk of Vanna's ass. Okay?"

"Sure, Grandpa."

Watching the shows, grandpa got a whiff of something he hadn't smelled in years.

"What do you suppose grandma's cooking up tonight," he asked Frankie. "Sure smells good."

"Sure does," Frankie said. "I'm getting hungry just smelling it."

"Turn that TV off, boys. Time for dinner," Grandma announced. "Go get washed up."

Doing as they were told, they washed up and headed to the kitchen.

"Hmmm, smells like corned beef and cabbage," Grandpa said. "I bet there's potatoes and carrots, too."

"Mom makes this all the time," Frankie said.

Sure enough, once they sat down at the table, there was a big bowl of corned beef and cabbage with carrots and potatoes sitting in the middle of the table.

"We must've done something right, kiddo. Ain't had this meal in a coons age. Dig in."

Frankie didn't need to be told twice.

The three of them ate in silence for a while when Grandpa said, "Say, kiddo, why don't we take a walk to the park tomorrow, and you can show me what kind of shortstop you really are."

"Can we," Frankie asked. "Are we allowed?"

"Course we can. The Huskers won't be back in town for a few days yet."

"Oh boy, you're the bestest grandpa."

At that moment, Grandma felt happier than she had in years. Who knew that having Frankie around would bring about such a change in her husband? A thought began to formulate in her head, but she wouldn't let the two of them in on her little secret yet.

Chapter - 9

The next morning, Grandpa woke up early enough to catch the sunrise. Dressed and ready to face the day, he walked out to the porch only to find his old Louisville Slugger baseball bat leaning against his rocker. Ain't seen that in too long to remember, he thought. What's that woman up to?

Wrack his brain as he might, he couldn't come up with any answers. He decided to load his pipe and enjoy the sunrise.

During breakfast, all Frankie could talk about was playing on a professional baseball field. His dreams, the night before, were filled with the glory of being a baseball star.

He had hardly touched his food when his grandma said, "No baseball until you finish your breakfast."

After that rebuke, Frankie ate everything on his plate and announced that he would help with the dishes.

All Grandpa could do was watch in awe at the wonderment of youth. The energy, the hopes, and dreams. All that seems to fade in the face of reality. Work, family, medical issues. They slowly eat away at any hope of fulfilling your dreams. The only thing I ever wanted was a happy life with the woman I love. But I sure made a mess of that, he thought.

"GRANDPA!" Frankie yelled with excitement and anticipation.

Coming back to reality, Grandpa shook his head and stared at Frankie.

"When can we go to the park," Frankie asked.

"Right," Grandpa said. "I'm ready whenever you are."

"Great, I'm almost done with the dishes," Frankie stated.

"Sure, kiddo, see you on the porch."

Once Frankie finished the dishes, he hurriedly kissed his grandma on the cheek, grabbed his glove and met Grandpa on the porch.

Grandpa had his glove in one hand and his Louisville Slugger in the other.

Surprised to see that his grandpa had a bat, Frankie said, "I didn't know you had a bat, grandpa."

"Had this thing for years, kiddo. I used to play a bit when your mom was younger," Grandpa replied as he lovingly caressed his Louisville Slugger and thought about the last time he used it. Been too long, he thought. "Alright, kiddo, let's get to the park and see what ya got."

With that, Frankie and Grandpa headed out for a morning of bonding through baseball.

"Can I carry the bat," Frankie asked.

"Sure, kiddo," he replied. "But ya gotta do it right. What you do is slip the glove on the bat and carry the bat on your shoulder."

Doing as he was told, Frankie asked, "Like this grandpa?"

"Just like that," he replied. And off they went to the park.

Meanwhile, as Grandma was finishing up in the kitchen, the phone rang. Who could that be, she thought? Drying her hands, she went to answer the phone.

"Hello," she said.

"Hi, mom. It's me," Elaine said on the other end. "How are you?"

"I'm just fine, dear," she replied. "How are things with the new job?"

"They're wonderful," Elaine said. "I'm getting used to the way things work around here."

"I'm so happy for you, dear."

"Listen, Mom. I just called to see how things were going with Frankie. Is he behaving himself?"

"Yes, dear," her mother replied. "He's been a breath of fresh air around here."

"That's great to hear, Mom. I need to leave for work in a few minutes. Can I talk to Frankie?"

"Frankie isn't here, dear."

"Not there," Elaine said. "Where could he possibly be?"

"He went to the park to play baseball."

"With who?" Elaine asked with a bit of puzzlement in her voice.

"Your father, of course," her mom said.

"FATHER," Elaine shouted. "How could that be possible?"

"Your father and Frankie have become like two peas in a pod. They've been spending a lot of time together. It's amazing, really," her mother said.

"Will wonders never cease," Elaine said, her voice dripping with sarcasm.

"Frankie has been good therapy for everyone," her mom said.

"If you say so, mom. Well, I better get going. Tell Frankie I miss and love him, please."

"Of course, dear. Don't work too hard. I love you."

"Love you too, mom."

Hanging up the phone, Grandma couldn't help but smile at the way things were changing for the better. I think I'll make some sandwiches for the boys and see how they're doing at the park, she thought.

Meanwhile, Frankie and his grandpa were at the park warming up with a few tosses back and forth. "Are you ready, kiddo," grandpa asked.

"You bet. Let's get going."

"Hey, kiddo. Run over to the dugout and grab two of those buckets of balls."

Frankie did as Grandpa asked in record time. Dropping the two buckets on home plate, he ran out to the shortstop position.

Grandpa hit a soft grounder right to Frankie, who fielded it with ease.

It continued on this way for a few minutes when Frankie got frustrated and yelled, "C'mon, grandpa. Hit the ball harder. Make me run for them." After a beat, he added, "Show me what you got."

Grandpa smiled and said, "Okay, kiddo."

And proceeded to change the speed and locations of the grounders he was hitting to Frankie. The kid is pretty good, he thought.

After about 30 minutes of hitting, Grandpa was getting tired. So, he asked Frankie if he wanted to get in some batting practice.

"Oh boy. Yes, sir," Frankie replied.

Frankie grabbed the bat and was surprised at how light it felt. He looked at the bottom of the handle and saw the number 27. He knew that meant the bat weighed 27 ounces. Two ounces more than the one he uses at school.

Frankie took his position at the plate, and Grandpa delivered his first pitch.

Crack went the bat as Frankie connected with the ball and sent it down the third-base line.

"Not bad, kiddo," Grandpa said.

They continued this way for another 30 minutes or so when Frankie announced that he was thirsty.

"There's some bottles of coke in the cooler in the dugout kiddo. Let's take a break and sit in the shade."

"Okay, Grandpa."

Once in the dugout, Frankie reached into the cooler and was surprised to find not only Coke but Tab, too.

"Did Mom tell you that I liked Tab the bestest?" he asked.

"Nope," Grandpa replied as he thought back to how Elaine thought Tab was the bestest, too. This kid, sure as shootin', is just like his mother.

"Say, kiddo, where'd you learn how to play baseball," Grandpa asked.

"Our PE teacher at school teaches us. He's also our coach."

"Well, you sure learned how to play right good. You're really quick to react when I hit the ball. They'd say you have fast reflexes. You're hitting ain't so bad either."

"Thanks, Grandpa."

But his grandpa didn't hear him; he was busy looking at the darkening sky. This ain't looking good, he thought. I hope this ain't a twister comin' on. Too far to go to get home now, he thought.

Looking at his grandpa, Frankie could sense something was wrong.

"What are you looking at, Grandpa," he asked.

"Sky is getting dark, kiddo. Looks like we might be getting some rain."

Just then, Frankie saw his grandma walking into the park carrying a picnic basket.

"Look, Grandpa, here comes Grandma."

Grandpa was surprised to see his wife. He could tell by the picnic basket that they were in for a good lunch.

"Run out and grab that basket from grandma, kiddo."

Frankie ran to his grandma and grabbed the basket.

"I'll carry this," he said.

"Aren't you just the perfect gentleman," she said.

When Grandma and Frankie got back to the dugout, Grandpa asked Grandma if she had heard anything about the weather changing.

"I didn't hear any news today. I was busy baking."

"Well," Grandpa said. "By the looks of that sky, we may be in for a rough ride. Should be okay if we stay in the dugout."

"Oh dear. And us with no umbrellas," she said.

"What's happening, Grandpa," Frankie asked.

"Well kiddo, looks like we might be getting a twister around these parts. Sooner than later, I'm thinking."

"I'm scared, grandpa."

"Me too, kiddo, but if we stay right here, we should be okay. Nothing to worry about."

"That's right, Frankie. Grandpa knows best in these situations. We'll be fine. In the meantime, let's have some lunch. I made some meatloaf sandwiches on freshly baked bread with mayo and some potato salad, and I brought some iced tea as well. Are you boys hungry?"

"I sure am," Frankie replied as he reached into the basket for a sandwich.

His grandma pushed his hand away and proceeded to take out three dishes and put a helping of potato salad on each. She then took out the sandwiches, which she wrapped in wax paper.

Plates and glasses full, they settled into a comfortable silence. Grandma was smiling as she watched Frankie eat his lunch, and Grandpa kept himself busy watching the darkening sky.

When the first few raindrops fell, Grandpa knew exactly what was coming. It was just a matter of where it was going to make landfall. The air was heavy with moisture, the wind had picked up considerably, and the clouds were so dark that it looked like everything was a shadow moving with the wind.

"Let's move down to the other end of the dugout," Grandpa said. "We'll be protected better from the wind down there."

With a flash of lightning and a booming thunder directly overhead, the rain began to fall. Slowly at first, with drops that, when they hit the ground, turned into perfect circles on the dirt around the infield.

The rain started to come down in sheets that seemed to move sideways with the wind. Frankie had never experienced a storm like this.

"Grandpa, is this a twister?"

"Not yet, kiddo. Do you know what a twister looks like?"

"Yes, sir."

"Good. Keep your eyes open for anything that might look like a twister to you."

That being said, Grandpa wrapped his arms around Frankie and his wife. I hope this thing turns before it gets here, he thought.

Surprisingly, the rain stopped, and the sky turned blue faster than you could close an umbrella. Grandpa walked out of the dugout to survey the damage. Nothing but a few loose signs on the fences, and a garbage can got knocked over, leaving trash all over the infield.

"We got lucky," Grandpa said. He turned around to tell Frankie to start picking up the trash, but Frankie was already on the field with a trash bag in hand.

Shaking his head, Grandpa yelled to Frankie, "Try to get everything you can, kiddo."

"I will, Grandpa," Frankie replied.

"Once we get all the trash picked up, I guess we can head home. The field is too wet to get any more practice in today," Grandma stated.

"Really, Grandma?" Frankie whined.

Before Grandma could answer, Grandpa voiced his agreement, and the three of them proceeded to pick up the remaining trash.

When they were finished, Grandpa grabbed the picnic basket and said, "The last one home is a monkey's uncle."

Frankie took off immediately and never looked back. His grandparents laughed as Grandpa grabbed the picnic basket in one hand and held the other out to his wife. Surprised at this gesture, she hesitated, but only for a second. They held hands all the way home as they walked in a comfortable silence. Each in their own thoughts. She realized that this small gesture of affection was one of the things she had been missing.

Chapter - 10

Once back at the house, Grandpa said, "Thanks for bringing lunch down to the park, Marge. It was right, fine. I wonder where Frankie is hiding."

"He's probably watching Vanna's ass," Grandma said with a laugh. "You sure are teaching him the finer things in life, Steve. Could be worse, I guess."

"I may watch Vanna's ass, but I watch it because she's got the only ass that even comes close to yours."

Turning bright red, Grandma said, "You're incorrigible," and walked into the house with a huge smile on her face

Back in the kitchen, Grandma was preparing to cook dinner when Grandpa announced from the bathroom that he was treating everyone to a meal out.

"Where are we going, Grandpa?" Frankie asked as he joined him in the bathroom.

"It's a secret, kiddo. It's your grandma's favorite restaurant. She deserves a night off, don't you think so, kiddo?"

"She does work hard every day," Frankie said.

"Keep this between us, kiddo. I want grandma to be surprised."

"Okay, Grandpa."

"Hey, Marge," Grandpa said.

"Yes, Steve?

"Make sure to wear that blue dress I like."

"Why the blue one," she asked.

"Vanna ain't got nothing on you," he replied with a silly smirk on his face.

Bringing his voice down to a whisper, he said to Frankie, "I always did love your grandma's ass, kiddo. The blue dress makes her look like a princess. I bet she even wears her pearls tonight."

When the boys were finished in the bathroom, Grandma rushed past them and shut the door.

"I'll be out in a few minutes. Why don't you two wait on the porch?"

"She ain't never been out in a few minutes, kiddo. We might as well get comfortable while she's getting gussied up."

"Gussied up?"

"You know, kiddo. Makeup, hair, nails etc. If I were a betting man, I'd bet she'd be out in twenty-five minutes. What's your guess, kiddo?"

"Twenty-nine minutes. You keep track, Grandpa. Starting now. Wait a minute, what are we betting?"

"Well, the one closest to the time will be the winner. If you win, I'll take you to town tomorrow and get you a new bat. How does that sound, kiddo?"

"That sounds great! Hey, wait a minute. What if you win?"

"I'll go see a Huskers game with you, and you can buy one of those fried bologna sandwiches for me. Deal?"

Grandpa and Frankie shook on the deal and waited until Grandma was finished.

After what seemed like hours, Grandma walked out to the porch. Dressed in a blue dress and wearing her pearl necklace.

"How long, Grandpa?"

"Just hit thirty minutes, kiddo. You win."

"Win what," Grandma asked.

"Just a gentlemen's bet between me and Frankie. He just won a brand-new baseball bat."

"What did you bet on?" she asked.

"You, Grandma!" Frankie blurted out before Grandpa could shush him up.

"Me, what on earth for?"

"We bet on how many minutes you would take in the bathroom. I guessed 29, so I won. Grandpa was right, you do look like a princess in that dress. Look, Grandpa, she's wearing the pearl necklace just like you said she would."

Grandma looked at Grandpa with a sly smile and kissed him on the forehead.

"Thank you, Steve. You're wearing my favorite outfit. I don't know what's gotten into you, but I LOVE IT."

Looking somewhat embarrassed, Grandpa mumbled a thank you and said, "Time to head out. I made reservations for 6:30."

Piling into the 65 wagon, they headed out to a surprise dinner.

This was an adventure for Frankie. He had never been to a restaurant in the city they were going to.

"How long before we're there, Grandpa?"

"Not long, kiddo. We'll need to find a place to park first."

Spotting a parking space across the street, Grandpa made a U-turn and slid right into it.

"Everyone ready?"

"Where's the restaurant, Grandpa?"

Pointing across the street, Grandpa said, "Right there. Ivan the Kozak makes the best perogies in these parts. Is this okay, Marge?"

"It's my favorite. Of course, it's okay," she said.

Crossing the street, they walked into the restaurant and were greeted with the aromas of another world. Frankie couldn't decide what he was smelling, but he knew it had to be delicious.

"What kind of food do they have here, Grandpa?"

"Eastern European but mostly Russian," Grandpa replied.

"Wow. I've never had Russian food before."

Just then, the hostess greeted them and asked if they wanted smoking or non.

"Non," Grandma said. "By the window if possible."

Walking through the restaurant to their table, Frankie was amazed at the decorations on the walls and ceiling. On the walls, there were hunting scenes and pictures of castles in clouds. From the ceiling hung pieces of colorful cloth with designs that Frankie had never seen.

"This place is the bestest. I'm hungry. Can we order?"

The hostess had left menus on the table. They picked them up to read through them when Frankie announced to the whole place that there was too much to choose from.

"I can't make up my mind."

A few minutes later, a waitress approached the table to take their orders. Grandma ordered the Halupki or stuffed cabbage with mashed potatoes. Grandpa had the rabbit stew and Frankie ordered potato pancakes with a side of sliced kielbasa. As an afterthought, Grandma ordered a variety of pierogies.

While waiting for their dinner to arrive, Frankie was too engrossed in the décor of the place to carry on much of a conversation. Grandma was still in shock about going out to eat, and Grandpa was thinking how much he wanted to smoke his pipe.

After what seemed like hours, the food arrived hot and steaming.

"This is marvelous, Steve. Thank you so much. It's been years since we came here."

"Oh, ain't been that long, Marge. Just seems like it."

"Doesn't really matter," she said. "It's just as I remembered it. Thank you!"

"I wonder if the same guy is cooking?" Grandpa said.

"Who cares," Frankie said through mouthfuls of potato pancakes.

"I agree," Grandma said. "Let's just enjoy our meals."

With that, they dug in and devoured their food like they hadn't had a decent meal in weeks.

"Well," Grandpa stated, "That was worth the trip to the city."

"Steve, it was only a 20-minute ride, and this is the only place worth eating at."

"Still, I haven't worn a tie in too many years. Would it be okay if I took it off now?"

"No, it's not okay. We're still in the restaurant. At least wait until we walk out the door."

"See, kiddo, this is what happens when you're married as long as Grandma and I are. Everything must go through the wife. Isn't that right Marge?" he said with a grin as he put his arms around both of them.

Marge put her head on his shoulder and Frankie stopped to look in the window of the sporting goods store.

Unfortunately, the store was closed so Frankie had to wait to get his new bat.

"Want to take a walk around and enjoy the night?" Grandpa asked.

"Are you sure that you're up to it, Steve? You've had a big day. Oh, and you can take that tie off now."

"That's a relief. I could hardly breathe with that thing around my neck."

They walked in silence until they reached the end of Main Street, then turned around and headed back to the car.

"That was great, Grandpa. Thanks for treating us to dinner."

"Don't mention it, kiddo. If we hurry, we might still be able to catch the crow's sunset serenade tonight."

"Yeah," Frankie said. "Let's make them sing real loud tonight."

The three of them laughed out loud to that one and settled in for the ride home.

They drove in silence for a few miles when Grandpa asked Frankie, "What kind of bat are you thinking of getting, kiddo?"

Getting no response, he checked in the rearview mirror and could see that Frankie was out for the count.

Smiling, he said to his wife, "Remind you of someone else?"

His wife turned to look at a sleeping Frankie and was surprised to see the uncanny resemblance he had to his mother at that age.

With a sad smile on her face, she asked, "Where did we go wrong, Steve?"

"What do you mean?"

"You know exactly what I mean."

"I'm guessing I do. I don't know where to start, Marge."

"Let me help. The letters."

Steve winced as if hit in the gut and felt the wind go out of his sails.

"I wished I had never found them, let alone read them."

"But you did read them and said some awful things."

"That's true. And for that, I am truly sorry. I never wanted to hurt you or Elaine. Thinking back, I probably knew all along Elaine wasn't mine. But she is mine, or at least she was until she heard us arguing that night. Then, I disappeared for two days with no word if I was dead or alive. I hate myself for hurting the people I love most. You've been the perfect wife. Nobody could ask for more. I've lost 25 years to my stubborn pride. I don't want to lose any more Marge. I know forgetting is out of the question. Can you ever forgive me, though?"

"Oh Steve, I've waited so long for this. Of course, I forgive you. You know I have always loved you. Stubborn pride and all. Is this what you wanted to set straight?"

"This is just the start. The hard part is next."

Looking at each other, they said in unison, "Elaine."

They made the rest of the ride home, each in their own thoughts, in silence.

Pulling up to the house, Grandpa cut the engine and looked at his wife, "I know I hardly say it, but I love you, Marge. Always have, always will."

Getting out of the car, Grandma said, "I'll wake Frankie so he can walk in."

"No need," Grandpa said. "I can carry him."

Opening the back door, he scooped up Frankie in his arms and walked toward the house.

"Are you sure, Steve? He's not an infant anymore."

"I'll be fine, woman. Now get inside and don't forget your bag. Maybe a little something to eat before bed would be good."

"If you're sure. Just don't hurt yourself."

With that, Grandpa carried Frankie to his room, changed him into his pajamas and laid him in bed. I don't think he ever woke up, Grandpa thought. We had a big day. I'm pretty tired myself.

"Goodnight, kiddo,' he whispered as he kissed Frankie's forehead. "Thank you for helping me to set things straight."

"Are things going to be okay, Grandpa," Frankie asked in a sleepy voice.

"Right as rain, kiddo, right as rain."

Chapter - 11

The next morning, Frankie woke up and immediately thought, I'm getting my own bat today, He raced out to the kitchen, ready to remind his grandpa about the bat, but there was no one there. Strange, he thought.

"Hey. Where is everybody," he yelled.

"Be right there," his grandma called back. "There's juice in the fridge. Please pour three glasses."

"Okay," he said. Wondering why his grandma and grandpa were still in bed after 8.

Frankie got three glasses from the counter and the juice from the fridge. He poured the juice, drank his half in one swallow, and refilled his glass.

"I saw that young man," his grandma said from behind him.

Grinning sheepishly, he said, "Sorry, Grandma."

"Your mother used to do the exact same thing."

"She still does," Frankie said with a big grin.

Smiling, his grandma asked, "Now, what would you like for breakfast?"

"Anything?" Frankie asked.

"If we have it in the house, I'll make it."

"How about a ham steak, eggs and some potatoes," he said.

Looking in the fridge, his grandma said, "You're in luck. We have a nice thick ham steak in here. Why don't you go get the paper for your grandpa and wait on the porch until breakfast is ready?"

"Sure, grandma."

And he ran out of the house to get the paper from the mailbox.

Where do they get all their energy from? she thought. After yesterday and last night, both she and Grandpa could have used an extra hour in bed. Oh well, she thought as a sly grin spread across her glowing face.

Frankie was sitting impatiently for his grandpa to get out to the porch so they could read how the Huskers were doing.

"That corn sure is getting bigger," he said to no one in particular.

"Sure is, kiddo," Grandpa said as he walked out the door and sat in his chair.

"Morning, Grandpa. Are you feeling okay?"

"Real fine, kiddo, real fine," he replied as he thought about last night. Well, let's just keep that thought for later.

"Here's your paper, Grandpa. I waited for you before I read the sports section."

"That's right, nice of you, kiddo, but I think from now on, you don't have to wait for me anymore."

"Gee, thanks, Grandpa."

"Sure, kiddo. Now, how are our Huskers doing?"

"I'll look." Frankie found the sports section and began to read to himself.

Grandpa said, "Why don't you read it out loud? Let's see how you can read. Don't be afraid if you don't know a word. I'll help you out."

"Sure, Grandpa. Here goes. The Huskers win again, it says. They swept a 3-game series from the Omaha Crows. Wow, they won 16-5. Their hitting has really improved."

"Sounds that way. What place are they in now?" Grandpa asked.

"Second place. Only two games out of first."

"Hmmm, not bad."

"Not bad! Grandpa, that's great!"

"Okay, kiddo, It's great!"

Just at that moment, Grandma called them in for breakfast

They both stood up and headed into the kitchen when Grandpa said, "You go ahead kiddo. I'll be right there."

"Okay," Frankie said and ran up to his grandma and gave her a big hug. "You're the bestest grandma ever."

"Why, thank you, dear. You're the bestest grandson ever," she said with a big smile.

Frankie had just sat down when Grandpa walked in and handed him a box.

"This used to be your mother's. Thought you might like it."

"Gee, thanks, Grandpa. What is it?"

"You know how to read, don't ya? Read the box."

As Frankie started to read the box, Grandma looked back to see what box he was talking about. She was surprised when she saw what it was.

"Where in the world did you find that husband?" she asked.

"I found it in the shed in a box of some of Elaine's old stuff."

"I didn't know there were any boxes out there," she replied with a quizzical look on her face.

"We put a few out there when Elaine took off. I forgot all about them until Frankie found that baseball card."

"Well, what else was there?"

"Not much. Just some junk. That was the only thing worth anything to anyone. I'm setting things right, Marge. You should know that from the talk we had early this morning."

"I see. Well, you can look at that later, Frankie. Eat your breakfast before it gets cold. I'm sure you're excited about getting a new bat today. So, eat up. The two of you."

"Yes, ma'am," they both said at the same time and laughed.

After breakfast, Frankie offered to help with the dishes, but his grandma insisted; they went outside and finished the paper before they left to go shopping while she cleaned up.

Frankie and Grandpa did as they were told and went out to the porch.

Once they were settled in their respective spots, Frankie asked, "What time are we leaving Grandpa?"

"Not for a while yet, kiddo. Stores don't open till round ten in these parts."

"Where are we going, Grandpa?"

"Out past Hogs Holler. About 2 hours' drive from here."

"Want to start on your puzzle, Grandpa?"

"Good idea, kiddo. Hand me that section right there."

"Here you go, Grandpa."

"Thanks, kiddo."

Time was passing too slowly for Frankie. He was too excited to read the paper. All he could do was think about that bat. He got up and walked over to the cornfield, looking for any crows he might be able to scare off. Having no luck on that front, he went and sat back down on the steps and heaved a big sigh.

"AAAAHHHH!"

Chuckling, Grandpa asked, "What's wrong, kiddo?" Knowing full well exactly what was wrong.

"Nothing. Just bored."

"I see. Sure you're not just excited?"

"Maybe that, too, a little," he said as his face turned bright red.

"Me too, kiddo. Me too. We'll be leaving real soon. Grandma is almost finished cleaning up."

Right on cue, Grandma appeared at the door and announced it was time to leave.

"Righto," Grandpa said as he and Frankie headed to the car.

The next thing they knew, Grandma was running past them, saying, "Last one, there is a monkey's uncle."

They looked at each other, and Grandpa whispered, "Why don't we let Grandma win this time, kiddo?" and winked.

"Sure thing, Grandpa."

Once they were all in the car, Grandpa said, "I forgot how fast you could run, Marge. We never could've beat you today."

"Oh, pshaw! You two didn't even try."

"You surprised us, Grandma, that's all. Right, Grandpa?"

"She sure did kiddo. She's full of surprises lately."

"Looks who's talking. Just some junk and that box, huh?"

Hearing that, Frankie remembered leaving the box on the table.

"I forgot the box," he said.

"It'll be there when you get back, kiddo. Time's a wastinge."

"Okay, Grandpa. Where are we going to eat lunch, Grandma?"

"I think there's still a Woolworths over there. Right, Steve?"

"Sure is. I think they still have the lunch counter and the balloons for the banana splits."

"What do balloons have to do with banana splits?" Frankie asked.

"You'll see kiddo. You'll see."

"Ok, Grandpa."

In no time at all, Frankie was sound asleep in the back seat again. Not a bad thing, Grandpa thought. The ride is boring. Nothing but cornfields and telephone poles.

They rode on in comfortable silence, each in their own thoughts, happier than they'd been in years.

Grandma woke Frankie up when they were almost in town.

"We're almost there, Frankie. Wake up"

Sitting up and yawning, he said, "I wasn't sleeping, Grandma. I was just resting my eyes."

"I guess that wasn't you snoring in the back seat then. Steve, did we bring any little piggies with us today?"

"Not that I recall," he replied.

"I don't snore, do I, Grandpa?"

"You sound like a little piggie," Grandma said.

"Do I, Grandpa?"

"'Fraid so kiddo. Sorry. You do sound like a little pig, though."

They all laughed at that one as Frankie announced that his mother said the same thing about his snoring. That just brought on more fits of laughter from all of them.

"The stores will be open by now, I reckon," Grandpa said. "Where to first wife?"

"I think I'll go to the shoe store first, then on to Sears to pick up some summer clothes for Frankie."

"Aw, Grandma. Quit kidding around. You know where Grandpa means."

"That I do, kiddo, that I do," Grandpa said as he maneuvered the Chevy wagon around a big ole John Deere. "Look at the size of that combine kiddo. Sure is a beautiful sight."

"It is big, but why is it beautiful?"

"Well, Frankie, when we start seeing these big boys out and about, we know that the corn is about ready for harvesting."

"Wow! Will I get to see the harvest?"

"Maybe, kiddo, maybe."

After what seemed like an eternity, Grandpa finally parked the car right in front of the sporting goods store.

Frankie was out the door in a flash when his grandma said, "Slow down, Frankie. Wait for us old folks."

"Sorry, Grandma. I'll wait. But you're not old."

Grandpa got to the store's door first and held it open for Grandma and Frankie as he said, "After you, fair maiden and squire."

Grandma blushed and said, "Thank you, fine sir."

Frankie asked them both, "Why are you talking so funny?"

"We're just kidding around, dear," replied his grandma.

"Can we just go inside and look around, please?"

"Frankie's right, Marge. This is serious stuff we're doing today. Lead us to the treasure then."

Shaking his head, Frankie walked past both of them and said, "People your age sure do act funny sometimes."

"That we do, kiddo, that we do," Grandpa said.

"There's the baseball stuff over there," Frankie said and raced down the aisle.

Stopping in his tracks, Frankie looked in awe at the selection of bats.

He picked one up and almost dropped it when Grandpa caught it and said, "That one's a bit heavy for you, kiddo. Look for a 27- or 28-ounce bat."

"Okay."

Frankie inspected the bats and found that they were arranged according to size, from smallest to biggest. Walking down the aisle a few feet, he found what he was searching for.

"Here they are, Grandpa. There are so many different kinds. How do I know which one is right?"

"Well, kiddo, just pick one up and see how it feels when you swing."

Frankie did just that and picked up the bat closest to him. He got a serious look on his face as he took a few practice swings. Shaking his head, he put the bat back and couldn't decide which one to try next. Grandpa reached in, grabbed a bat and handed it to Frankie.

"I always liked the Louisville Slugger myself. Try this one out."

Frankie grabbed it and got that serious look on his face again.

"Who's pitching today, Kiddo?" Grandpa asked.

Not missing a beat, Frankie said, "Nolan Ryan. He's the bestest pitcher in baseball."

"Well, how does that bat feel?" Grandma asked.

After a few more swings, Frankie announced, "This is it. It feels right."

Looking at the bottom, he noticed it was a 29-ounce bat.

He showed his grandpa, who said, "You seemed to handle that fine kiddo. If it feels right, you can't say no. Now, let's go and see about getting you some new cleats. Maybe a few other things, too."

By the time they finished shopping, Frankie had a new bat, cleats, balls and a Corn Huskers warm-up jacket and hat. He couldn't believe how lucky he was.

"Wait until I tell Mom about all the new stuff I got."

"I bet she'll be jealous," Grandma said.

"Maybe," Frankie said. "I'm starving. Can we eat lunch now?"

"Sure, kiddo," Grandpa said. "Let's put all this stuff in the car first, and then we can go grab a bite at Woolworth's."

"If you don't mind, I'll wait here for you two," Grandma said.

"Sure, Grandma, we'll be right back."

Grandpa and Frankie walked hand in hand to the car and loaded everything into the back of the Chevy wagon.

Grandma watched as they completed their task. With a smile and a nod, she felt that a huge weight had been lifted off her shoulders.

Chapter - 12

The three of them walked hand in hand to Woolworth's. When they walked in, the lunch counter was directly to the left. The aromas coming from the grill were making Frankie's stomach growl so loud that his grandma heard.

"Sounds like we have a hungry boy on our hands, Steve. Let's sit by the grill so Frankie can watch them cook our food," Grandma said.

They took their seats at the counter, and Frankie proceeded to push himself around in circles when his grandpa said, "I thought you said you were hungry. Sit still and look at the menu on the wall. Order anything you want, kiddo."

There were so many things on the menu that Frankie couldn't make up his mind.

"What are you going to get?" he asked.

"I'm thinking a grilled cheese and tomato soup. How about you, Marge?"

"That sounds good. I'll have the same," she replied. "How about you, Frankie?"

"I think I'll have a hot dog. Do you think they have fried onions?" he asked.

"I'm sure that can be arranged," Grandpa said.

The waitress just then walked up and said, "What'll you have?"

"The Mrs. and I will have a grilled cheese and tomato soup. Frankie?"

"I'd like a hot dog with fried onions, please, and an order of french fries."

"Anything to drink?" she asked.

"I think we'll all have chocolate shakes," Grandpa said.

The waitress read back their order loud enough so the cook could hear. He immediately started working on their order.

In no time at all, their lunch was ready and placed in front of them. They dug in as the conversation all but stopped.

Finishing first, Grandpa let out a loud burp.

"Steve," his wife said, "Not in public."

"In some countries, it's considered an insult to the chef if you don't burp," he replied.

"What countries are those?" she asked.

"Not quite sure. Just covering all the bases," said Grandpa with a grin.

Right then, Frankie let out a huge burp to rival his grandpa's.

"Excuse me," he said. "Just covering all the bases."

The waitress even had to laugh at that one. "Will there be anything else?" she asked.

"Do you still have room for dessert, kiddo?"

"Yes, sir. But maybe we can share a banana split."

"Good idea," Grandma said.

"We'll have one banana split with three spoons, please," Frankie said.

"Okay, kid. Pick a balloon," the waitress said.

"What for?" he asked.

"Just pick one kiddo, you'll see," his grandpa said.

"What's your favorite color?" the waitress asked.

"Orange. But I don't see any up there."

"There's one all the way down the other end of the counter. You want that one kid?"

"Yes, please."

The waitress, retrieved the balloon and handed it to Frankie.

"What do I do now?" he asked.

"Pop it," Grandpa said. "But first, you need to feel for a little piece of paper in the balloon and pinch it between your fingers. Find it?"

"I think so," Frankie said.

"Now, hold on to it while you pop it," Grandma said.

Frankie didn't understand what this had to do with a banana split, but he did as he was told. Squeezing the piece of paper between his fingers, he popped the balloon with his fork.

"Look at the paper now, kiddo."

Frankie unrolled the paper, revealing a number on it. "There's only a number on it," he said.

"What number is it," grandma asked.

"One," Frankie replied. "What does it mean?"

At that moment, the waitress chimed in, "It means you get the banana split for a penny, kid."

"No way," he said.

"Yes way," the waitress replied. "Be right back with your split."

"Is this true, Grandpa?"

"True as true can be kiddo."

The banana split arrived in a jiffy, and all three of them grabbed a spoon and dug in.

Frankie announced for all to hear, "I love you both. You're the bestest."

The waitress and cook both smiled at that one.

The ride back home began with lively chit-chat but soon ran to a comfortable silence as Frankie fell asleep again. Only this time, he was wearing his new Corn Husker hat and jacket, cradling the bat with a smile. Dreaming, I'm sure, of home runs and double plays, Grandpa thought.

"Well, wife, are you up to cooking tonight, or should we get fish and chips from that place right before Hogs Holler."

"Fish and chips sounds great. We haven't had it for years."

"Right then, fish and chips it is."

Frankie didn't even wake up when they stopped for fish and chips, so they got it to go.

Driving up the gravel driveway, Frankie woke up with a start. "Are we home already? What smells so good?"

"That would be the fish and chips we picked up on the way home," his grandpa said.

"I love fish and chips. Mom can make real good ones."

"That's nice, dear," Grandma said. "Why don't you run inside and get washed up."

"Leave all your stuff on the porch, and we'll check it out after dinner, kiddo."

"Okay, Grandpa." And off he ran into the house.

"That's a pretty good kid Elaine is raising. What do you think, Marge?"

"I think he's the best thing that has happened to us in a very long time."

"I can't argue with you there, wife. Let's get inside before the food gets cold."

In they went, holding hands and grinning like two school kids. Both realized that things were beginning to be right again. Grandma was hoping that things continued to get better, while Grandpa was just praying that his bum ticker lasted long enough to set things right with Elaine.

Grandma declared to everyone, "Since it's such a lovely evening, why don't we picnic on the porch tonight? Frankie, you grab the paper plates, napkins, and utensils. I'll take care of the drinks and food. Steve, you should just get in your rocker by Bassett and work on today's puzzle."

Frankie came out first with his stuff, followed closely by his grandma, who carried a tray with the food, a pitcher of iced tea, three glasses and lemon poppy seed cake for dessert.

Handing the tray to Grandpa, she spread out a small blanket she had been carrying over her shoulder.

Placing the food on the blanket just right and pouring the iced tea, she said, "Dig in, you two."

She sat down on the porch and dug in herself.

The three of them ate like they hadn't eaten in a week. The food was gone in record time. Grandma gathered up the dishes and asked Frankie to bring the blanket inside and put it in the laundry room.

After putting the blanket away, Frankie saw the box his grandpa had given him earlier. He decided to grab it and check it out on the porch.

When he got back out to the porch, Grandpa had arranged all of Frankie's new stuff in a neat pile.

"How about we go to the park tomorrow and see how that new bat works for you," Grandpa said.

"That would be great, Grandpa. All the stuff is the best. You're the best. Thank you, Grandpa." Then, yelling loud enough so Grandma could hear him in the house, he bellowed, "You're the best too, Grandma. I love you both."

Grandpa decided then and there that the first chance he got, he and Elaine would work things out as best they could. *I've missed too much over the years. I don't want to miss any more.*

"Say, it's getting late, kiddo. It's time for your bath and then bed. Sleep tight."

"Okay. I am pretty tired tonight. Thanks for a great day, Grandpa. Love you, goodnight."

Taking his box, he went inside.

After his bath, Frankie climbed into bed and waited for his grandma to come in and say good night. He used the time to examine the box. The name of the thing was 'SLINKY'. *That's a funny name for a toy,* he thought. Then he remembered that Mr. Whitiker used to be called Slinky. He had no idea what that might have to do with anything.

His grandma came in, and before he could ask her about the Slinky, she took the box and said, "Time for that tomorrow, dear. Sleep tight."

"I had a great time today, grandma."

"We did, too, Frankie. We love having you here. Both of us."

"I love being here, too. Good night, Grandma. Love you."

"Love you too dear."

Chapter - 13

The next morning, Frankie woke up to the smell of waffles. Oh boy, he thought and raced to the bathroom to brush his teeth. When he was finished, he ran back to his room and opened the box from his grandpa. In it, he found the strangest thing. When he took it out of the box, it began to stretch like a spring, with half remaining in the box and the other half in Frankie's hand. This is pretty neat, he thought. He turned the box upside down, and the remaining Slinky fell into his other hand. He decided to wear it as a bracelet and ask his grandpa what this thing does.

Once in the kitchen, Grandpa was in his usual chair reading the paper.

"It says here that the Huskers are coming back home for the last two games of the season," Grandpa said.

"When is that?" Frankie asked.

"They have two games left to play in Omaha and will be back here on Saturday for a doubleheader. If they win both games in Omaha, they'll be tied for first place."

"Wow, that means they can win the pennant but have to win both halves of the doubleheader. What happens if they split the games, Grandpa?"

"I seem to recall one year, a long time ago, the same thing happened, and they scheduled one game to decide the championship," Grandpa said. "That could happen this year, kiddo."

"I know. I can't wait to go watch the games on Saturday."

"I'm starving kiddo. How about you?"

"Me too. Hey, Grandma, how long before we can eat?"

"I'm bringing over the waffles right now. You can start on the bacon and hash browns sitting right there in front of you."

Sure enough, the potatoes and bacon had magically appeared on the table. Both Frankie and Grandpa finished loading their plates when Grandma brought a steaming plate of waffles with a fresh stick of butter on the side.

"Now we can eat," she declared.

After finishing breakfast, Grandma shooed Grandpa and Frankie away and told them to enjoy the morning.

Out on the porch, they settled into their usual positions and started watching the corn grow.

"The corn sure did grow a lot since I got here," Frankie said.

"Sure did, kiddo. In another week, maybe two, they'll be taking all this corn to the market."

"Can we go and pick some before that?"

"Sure, kiddo. How about right now? Before it gets too hot."

"Can we really?"

"Sure. Go inside and ask your grandma for a couple of bags of corn. I'll walk out to the field and meet you there."

Running to the house, Frankie shouted over his shoulder, "Okay, Grandpa."

When he got to the kitchen, he asked Grandma for some bags.

"What on earth for," she said.

"Grandpa said that we could go and pick some corn today. Want to join us?"

"Sounds like fun, but I have things to do. Here's your bags. Have fun."

"Thanks, Grandma. I'll even shuck them later for dinner."

Grabbing the bags, he headed back out to his grandpa, who was waiting right where he said he would be.

"Here they are. They're kind of big, so I guess Grandma wants us to pick a lot of corn."

"They sure are big. Maybe one bag will be enough," Grandpa said. "I'll keep the other one in my pocket just in case."

Grandma watched from the window as they walked into the corn. She couldn't see them but could tell where they were when the two of them scared some crows off. It's good to see Steve a little more active, she thought.

Once in the field, Frankie got a little scared because he couldn't see any way out.

"I'm scared, Grandpa," he said. "What if we get lost?"

"No chance of that kiddo. I've been around these fields all my life. You're in good hands."

"Okay. How do you know which ones to pick?"

"Well, I always look at the hairs coming out the end. If they're a nice light yellow with just a touch of brown at the end, they're ready for eating. Think you can handle that, kiddo?"

"You bet! Just watch me."

Frankie caught on quickly and could pick out the good ones at a glance.

"You're doing great, kiddo. Think we got enough for today." Looking in the bag, Grandpa said, "More than enough, I reckon. Let's head back now."

Frankie knew that his grandpa would never lose him and grabbed his hand as they walked toward the house.

The morning passed in the usual way. Just sitting with grandpa and talking baseball or doing the crossword puzzle. At lunchtime, Grandma brought out a couple of sandwiches and two ice-cold root beers.

"Thought you two might be getting hungry. It's nearly 1:30. I guess dinner will be a little later than usual tonight. Enjoy your lunch."

And she disappeared back into the house.

"Grandma sure takes good care of us."

"She sure does kiddo. I forgot how hard she works every day."

"Maybe you can do something nice for her."

"Like what, kiddo?"

"Well, Mom likes to go and get her nails done. I can't remember what she called it, though."

"Could it be a manicure or pedicure," Grandpa asked.

"YES! Both of those. Mom always comes home happy after she goes to the salon."

"Good idea, kiddo. I'll have to look into it. Say, the Huskers got that doubleheader in Omaha today. Keep your fingers crossed. This could be their year."

Just then, he looked down and saw the slinky on his arm.

"Hey, Grandpa. What does this thing do?"

"Not sure, kiddo."

"Why would Mom save this?"

"Don't know that either. Maybe you should ask her."

"I think I will. About the card, too."

"That's a fine idea, kiddo. A fine idea," but Grandpa was worrying about how the kid would take the news.

For dinner, there was corn on the cob, of course, some pulled BBQ pork, coleslaw, and cornbread.

They ate in silence until Frankie asked his grandma about the slinky, "Hey grandma, what exactly does this thing do?"

"Doesn't it have instructions," she asked.

"Nope, just a couple of pictures on the box."

"Maybe you should ask your mother," she said.

"Yeah, Grandpa suggested that, too. Is there something bad that happened a long time ago?"

"Say, kiddo, remember I talked about setting things straight." Frankie nodded, so Grandpa continued on, "This is all part of that. I promise you that before you go back home to your mom, all this will be fixed."

"Okay, Grandpa. I believe you."

They finished eating in silence, and Grandma and Frankie cleaned up. Grandpa decided to go to bed early, so he said good night, and off he went.

"Is Grandpa okay, Grandma?"

"Yes, dear. He's just a little tired from all the driving he's been doing lately. Nothing to worry about."

"Ok. I guess I'll wash up and go to bed, too. Love you, Grandma."

"Love you too, Frankie."

Chapter - 14

The next morning, Frankie got up early so he could get the newspaper for his grandpa. He ran all the way to the mailbox and back. He was out of breath when he made it to the kitchen.

"Where's Grandpa?"

"He's just running a little late today. Just put the paper down and pour juice for all of us, please."

"Sure, Grandma."

After pouring the juice and taking a big gulp, Grandma brought over some pigs in a blanket, home-fried potatoes, and rye toast.

"This looks great, Grandma. Thanks."

"You're welcome, dear."

Frankie was reaching for the food when he saw his grandpa walking into the kitchen.

He put his fork down and said, "You first, Grandpa. I can wait."

"That's right, nice of you, kiddo. You can start, though. I'm right behind you."

With their stomachs full and plates empty, all three of them were sitting back rubbing their bellies when Grandpa said, "I'm fuller than a tick on a dog."

Laughing, Frankie said, "I've never seen a real tick. Just pictures."

"They're ugly little things, and I despise them," Grandma said.

"They are ugly. No doubt about it," Grandpa replied. "Do you need any help cleaning up Marge?"

"I think I have it under control. Nice of you to ask, though, if you could help."

Smiling at her, he just nodded and grabbed the paper, "C'mon, Frankie. Paper ain't gonna read itself."

Racing past his grandpa, Frankie burst through the screen door with a bang and took his regular position on the porch.

Walking out the door, Grandpa handed Frankie the sports section and sat down in his rocker.

"Why don't you read to me again, kiddo."

"Sure Grandpa. Wow! The Corn Huskers swept the doubleheader yesterday. It says their offense is on fire, and the pitching is stellar."

"Well, what do you know? That means they are tied for first place and need to win both games on Saturday. Anything else we need to know, kiddo?"

"It says here that the Huskers will be returning by bus late tonight. They have an off day tomorrow, then the doubleheader on Saturday. It also says that the Huskers can end a long championship drought if they win. If they split the games, another game is already scheduled for next Tuesday."

"Well, let's hope they can pull it off," Grandpa said.

"I just know they can. Mr. Whitiker is a good manager."

"Yeah, well, let's just wait and see, kiddo. I think I'll work on my puzzle now."

"I thought that we were going to the park again to try my new bat out."

"I forgot to tell you, kiddo. There's some sort of function going on today, and tomorrow, they need to prepare the field for Saturday. Sorry about that."

"That's okay, Grandpa. At least I can go see the Huskers win the championship on Saturday."

"That you can kiddo, that you can."

That night after dinner, Grandpa, again, wanted to go to bed early. So, he kissed his wife, tussled Frankie's hair and headed off to bed.

"Is Grandpa going to be okay, Grandma?"

"He seems to be fine. He has an appointment to see his heart doctor next week. We'll find out then if anything is wrong."

"Maybe he's just worn out from all the exercise he's been getting," Frankie said in all seriousness.

"You may be right, dear. He certainly has been doing quite a bit more since you got here. It's good for him. He seems happy."

"Okay then," Frankie said. "We'll let Grandpa rest until tomorrow. Okay?"

"When did you get so smart, young man?"

"I guess just now," he replied with a big smile. "Maybe I should go to bed, too. Good night, Grandma. Love you."

"Good night, Frankie, and thank you."

"For what, grandma?"

"For being such a good grandson and caring so much about Grandpa. You're the bestest."

"Hey, you stole that from me." Looking rather embarrassed, he said, "That's okay though. I stole it from Mom."

He then ran to his room, laughing all the way.

He sure is just like his mother, she thought and decided it was her bedtime as well.

The next morning, Frankie walked into the kitchen and was surprised to see only two places set for breakfast.

"Where's Grandpa," he asked.

"He said something about the car needing some work. He took it to town so his friend could help him with it. He said it might take a while if they have to wait for any parts."

"Okay. What's for breakfast?"

"How about just some cereal today? We bought some of your favorites. There's Trix and Coco Puffs," she said.

"Trix, please. I love them."

"I know, your mother told me. Maybe I'll join you."

She went to the cabinet, got herself a bowl and joined Frankie in a bowl of Trix.

Frankie poured milk on his cereal while he said, "I didn't know you liked cereal, Grandma."

"Oh yes, your mother and I used to have cereal for breakfast all the time."

"I didn't know that. That's neat."

After breakfast was finished and the dishes washed and put away, Grandma said to Frankie, "You'll need to look after yourself until lunch. Don't worry; I'm not going anywhere. I just have some sewing that needs finishing. If you need anything, just holler."

"I'll be fine, Grandma. I'll go and get the paper so I can read the sports section, and then I can watch some game shows. I can even sit in Grandpa's comfy chair."

"You can sit wherever you want, dear. I'll be right in the other room if you need me."

"Okay, Grandma."

Frankie's stomach started grumbling something fierce. He looked up at the clock and saw that it was past lunchtime already. I think I'll go find Grandma and see if she wants to have some lunch.

On his way to check on his grandma, he was calling out to her, "Grandma, where are you? I'm hungry. Can we eat lunch now?"

From behind the closed door to the spare room, Frankie could hear her rustling around.

"Are you okay, Grandma?"

"Yes, dear. I'll be out in just a minute. Go in the kitchen and set the table for us please. We're having soup and sandwiches today."

"Okay, Grandma."

Frankie had finished setting the table and was sitting in his chair when Grandma walked in. It looked like she had been crying.

"Are you okay, Grandma? Why were you crying?"

"It's silly really. I found some old pictures and stuff I forgot we saved. Looking through them made me feel a little sad. So, I cried thinking about how fast the years have passed. I'm fine now, though. Let's eat."

"If you're sure that you're okay."

"I'm fine dear. I'll just heat up the soup while you get out the stuff for sandwiches."

After lunch, Grandma told Frankie that she still needed to finish up in the other room.

"Just a few more things to go through," she said. "Are you going to be okay by yourself again?"

"Of course, Grandma. I'm a big kid now. Maybe I'll even try out Grandpa's rocker while I do a puzzle."

With a sad smile, Grandma said, "You go right ahead and do that. Call me if you need anything."

"I will," he replied.

While Frankie was sitting in his grandpa's rocker, he had time to think about things. I wonder what has got Grandma so upset. I can't believe a few old pictures would make her cry. But Mom cries when she looks at old pictures too. It must be a woman thing, just like Grandpa said.

As dinner time approached, there were no sounds coming from the kitchen. That's odd, he thought. Grandma is usually cooking by now. I wonder what she is doing now.

"Hey, Grandma," he yelled. "What are you doing in there?"

"Sorry, dear. I must have dozed off. I'll be right there. Leftovers for dinner tonight. Okay?"

"I like leftovers. Is there still some meatloaf left? I can make a sandwich if there is."

"Take what you like out of the fridge, dear. Meatloaf sounds good, though."

Frankie was getting the stuff ready for dinner when Grandma walked into the kitchen, she looked better than before but still not great.

"Feeling better," he asked her.

"Much better now."

At that moment, the phone rang, and his grandma rushed to pick it up.

"Hello," she said.

"Marge, this is Steve. Looks like I'll be spending the night here."

"Is everything okay, Steve?"

"Right as rain," he said. "Is Frankie there? Of course, he is. Where else would he be?"

"He's right here. Want to talk with him?"

"Yeah, put him on."

"Frankie, your grandpa wants to talk to you."

He quickly grabbed the phone and said, "Hi, Grandpa. How's things?"

"Real good, kiddo, real good. Say, I just wanted to say have a good time at the games tomorrow. You can tell me all about it when I get home. Should be sometime after dinner, I reckon."

"Okay, Grandpa. I love you."

"Love you too kiddo. Now put your grandma back on the phone, please."

"Grandma, he wants to talk to you again."

Going into the other room, she picked up the other phone and yelled to Frankie.

"I got it," she said.

"Okay. Bye, Grandpa. See you tomorrow."

Hanging up the phone, Frankie went about the business of making himself a meatloaf sandwich.

Hearing Frankie hang up the other phone, she immediately asked her husband, "What's going on, Steve.?"

"Nothing Marge. I'm just a little tired from the ride. I'll be home tomorrow around dinner-time. Depends on when the part arrives from the warehouse."

"Okay, Steve. You take care and be careful on the way home."

"I will Marge. I love you darling."

With those four words she knew that things were indeed getting right again.

"I love you too, Steve. See you tomorrow."

"That you will, Marge, that you will."

Hanging up the phone she still had a feeling that something wasn't right. She couldn't quite put her finger on it, though. Maybe I'm just being silly, she thought. Joining Frankie in the kitchen, she made herself a meatloaf sandwich and joined him at the table.

"Grandpa said that he should be home tomorrow for dinner. You can tell him all about the games then."

"Neato," he said and devoured his sandwich. "You look tired, Grandma. I can clean up the dishes if you want to go to bed early."

Putting her dish in the sink, she said, "Thank you, dear. I think I'll take you up on the offer. Good night and don't stay up too late."

"I won't, Grandma. Good night. Love you."

"Love you too, Frankie. Never change."

Chapter - 15

Frankie woke up before the sun on game day. He was so excited that he barely touched his breakfast.

"The game doesn't start until 2 today," his grandma said. "It won't help if you keep looking at the clock. That makes time go by slower. Finish your breakfast and go watch some TV. In fact, take your breakfast into the other room so you can watch while you eat."

"Oh boy, can I? Mom doesn't let me watch TV while we eat. She says it's family time."

"Of course, dear. It'll be our secret. Now, go and enjoy your morning."

"Thanks, Grandma."

By the time Frankie finished breakfast, there were only a few hours left before he could go to the park and watch batting practice. He could hardly sit still. Maybe Mr. Whitiker will finally sign my card today.

He was watching some show that he really didn't understand when his grandma said to him, "It's about time for you to head to the park Frankie. Batting practice will start soon."

"Finally," he said. "Can I just eat lunch at the park, Grandma?"

"Of course, dear. I wouldn't want you to miss out on the bestest fried bologna sandwiches ever," she said with a grin.

"Yours are good too, Grandma. I'll see you later. I love you."

"Be careful, dear."

Frankie arrived at the park just as the Huskers were starting batting practice. He went up to buy a ticket, but Gladys just waved him through with a smile.

"Enjoy the game," she said.

"I will," he said. "Oh, thank you for letting me into all the games for free. You're the bestest."

And off he went.

Yep, that's Elaine's kid, alright, she thought.

Frankie went to his usual seat next to the dugout. Cap just happened to be standing on the top step smoking a cigarette.

"Hi, Mr. Whitiker. Your guys did really good on the road trip."

"Yeah, kid, they did. We still got two maybe three games more. I have to thank you for the advice you gave, kid. You made me realize that getting back to the basics works every time."

"Yeah, that's what my coach says too."

"He's a wise man. Listen and learn as much as you can from him."

"I will, sir. Good luck today."

"Thanks, kid. Enjoy the game. Stay close, though; I might need your advice again."

"I'll be right here, Mr. Whitiker."

Something about that kid makes me take a second look at everything. Hell, I didn't touch a drop of Hootch on the road trip. Now, if I could just quit the cigs, he thought.

The first game was a complete disaster from start to finish. The pitchers were a bit wild, and his guys only got one hit off a bush league pitcher. They were swatting at flies. The final score was 10-0.

Cap was not happy and he made it known to his players.

"That was the most god-awful performance I've ever seen," he said. "I am at a loss for words. Everybody into the clubhouse."

"Excuse me, Mr. Whitiker."

"Not now, kid. I need to talk to the boys."

"I was thinking about that," Frankie said.

Cap stopped dead in his tracks and asked, "What do you think I should do?"

"Well," Frankie started. "The guys know they played a lousy game. I'm sure they feel bad about it. Maybe you should just ask them what they think. Couldn't hurt."

"Hmmm, that's something to think about. Say, kid, want to come into the clubhouse and meet the guys."

"Gosh, can I?"

"Sure, kid. C'mon, I'll show you around."

Frankie followed Cap into the clubhouse and stopped dead in his tracks. He looked around the room and was amazed at the amount of equipment they had.

"There's so much stuff here. We sure could use some of this at our school."

"Yeah, the owners ain't afraid to spend the money when we're winning. Anyway, hey guys, listen up. This is the kid. Kid, these are the guys who just got one hit," and he turned and walked straight to his office.

Over his shoulder, he said, "Look around, kid. I'll be in my office. And, you guys," he said a little louder. "Listen to this kid. He's got more baseball smarts than all of you combined."

"Thanks Mr. Whitiker," Frankie said.

The guys weren't all that interested in talking to a kid, so Frankie wandered around looking at all the interesting stuff lying around.

He was about to leave when one of the players asked him, "You play ball, kid?"

"Sure do," he said. "I'm the starting shortstop for our school team."

"Maybe we should give him a uniform and put him in at short. Couldn't do any worse than you lot," Cap said with a hint of irony in his voice.

Frankie hadn't realized that Cap was behind him, so he jumped a little.

"Didn't mean to scare you, kid. I know that I can't use you as a player but, I've been thinking. How about you be our bat boy for this game."

"Oh boy, I would love that. You're the bestest, Mr. Whitiker."

"Slim, show the kid around the dugout. Make sure he knows what to do and where to stand."

"Sure, Cap. C'mon, kid, I'll show you around."

Slim was showing Frankie the ropes and said, "This isn't very difficult. We all have our own bats over here in the bat box. The player's number is on the end of the bat. Hand the right bat to the right player. If the player gets a hit, wait until the ball is dead and go out and pick up the bat and put it back in the box."

"That's it? I can do that with no problem."

"Okay, kid. I got to go use the little boy's room. The game is going to start in 10 minutes or so. See you, kid."

Frankie couldn't believe his luck. In the dugout for the whole game! Maybe today Mr. Whitiker will sign my card, he thought.

He had ten minutes before the guys came back out, so he looked at the bat box. He noticed that they were just thrown in there any old way. He decided to rearrange them in numerical order. That's better, he thought. I hope Mr. Whitiker likes it.

The team came out to warm up before the game. They did the usual stretches and wind sprints. Cap was just watching them and keeping his mouth shut. Let's see if the kid is right, he thought.

Cap looked at the batting box and asked Frankie, "Did you do this, kid?"

"Yes, sir," Frankie replied.

"Good job, kid."

Shouting to his players, Cap said, "Everybody get in here now."

The players thought they were finally going to get the famous Cap Whitiker tirade, so they were ready for bear.

After all the players were in the dugout, Cap said, "Everybody, down this end."

The players all crowded around Cap.

"Look at this bat box," he said. "See anything different?"

"It's arranged in numerical order," Slim said, "So what."

"Yes, it is. And that's my point. This kid comes in and does a very basic thing. He arranged the bats according to your uniform number. My point is, boys, don't forget the basics. They got you this far. I believe that you have two more wins in you. Now, Slim, you take the lineup card to the ump. Be nice to him this time. You almost got ejected before the game started the last time he was the home plate ump."

"Sure, Cap," Slim replied. "Sweet as pie."

"Don't be a smart ass, or you'll be riding the pines. Got it?"

"Yes, sir."

Frankie was so engrossed in what Cap was saying that he didn't hear Gladys calling him.

"Hey, kid," she yelled.

Frankie turned around and said, "Yes, ma'am."

"Would you tell Cap I need to talk to him before the game starts? It's important," she said.

"Okay. Hey, Mr. Whitiker, the ticket lady needs to talk to you. She says it's important."

"I got a game to manage." Shaking his head, he said, "I'll be right there, kid."

He saw Gladys waiting by home plate. She motioned for him to join her. He walked over to her, ready to give her a lesson in baseball etiquette.

Before he could open his mouth, she said, "I'm sorry to bother you during the game, but this can't wait."

He saw the look on her face and knew something bad had happened.

"What's up, Gladys?"

"Well, I just got a call from the kid's grandmother. His grandfather had a heart attack, and he's in the hospital in Omaha. I need to take care of him tonight. His grandmother doesn't want him to know anything yet. Okay?"

"Sure, I get it. Poor kid. Who's his grandfather? Do I know him?"

"Pernell," she started, "That's Marge and Steve's grandkid."

"Elaine's kid?" he asked, already knowing the answer.

"Yep. Now, be nice to him. He's a good kid and your grandson," she said.

Cap was speechless.

When he finally found his voice again, he said, "Don't you worry, Gladys. That kid is in good hands."

Hoping he was right, she went back to her booth and wondered just how she was going to handle this situation. Maybe Marge will have more news before the game ends, she hoped.

The game was a real battle until the seventh inning. Both pitchers were in form and throwing heat. Neither team had a hit yet. During the seventh-inning stretch Cap took Frankie aside and asked him what he would say to the team right now.

"Well, sir, …"

"Not to me, kid. To the team. Listen up, guys. The kid has something to say. Go ahead, kid."

Okay, here I go, he thought.

"I've been following you guys all season. When I first started watching you, none of you seemed to be having much fun. I think losing can be as much fun as winning. My mom always says, 'If you try your best, good things can happen.' I think that's what you guys need to do. Just go out and have fun and do your best."

"You heard the kid. Let's have some fun out there," Cap said.

The whole team cheered as they prepared to take their turn at bat. You could feel the energy. The chatter picked up as Slim got to the plate. Cap gave him the sign to swing at the first pitch if it was close to the plate. He called time and stepped out of the box to look at the pitcher.

Chuckling, he said to the catcher, "I own him starting right now."

The catcher said, "Yeah, right. I guess the first two strikeouts were just practice."

"Just have him put it near the plate. I'll take care of the rest," Slim said.

The catcher gave the sign. The pitcher went into his wind-up, and he threw a slider that hung up just a little too much. Slim swung and connected for a line drive to left field. He thought it was going to be a foul ball, so he didn't even run to first base. To everyone's surprise, most of all Slim, the ball stayed fair and barely made it over the left field fence for a home run.

Clapping his hands, he ran around the bases as fast as he could.

His teammates were on the top step of the dugout, waiting to congratulate him on his first big league home run. It couldn't have come at a better time, too.

That home run opened the floodgates, and the Huskers scored six more runs in the seventh and added eight more in the eighth. The final score was 15-0. The other team never even got a hit, and only two players reached first base.

It was a masterclass in good, solid, basic baseball.

"Great job, guys," Cap yelled. "We still got one more to go. Stay focused, and get some rest tomorrow. Be here bright and early Monday morning. No later than 8 am."

"Thanks for your help today, kid. You did well. Can you help us out again on Tuesday?"

"I sure can, Mr. Whitiker. I'll see you at the practice on Monday."

"Okay, kid."

Frankie left the field at full gallop. Running right past Gladys, he was on his way to tell Grandma about the games when he heard his name.

"Hey Frankie, slow down, will ya."

"Yes, ma'am," he said. "Sorry."

"No need to apologize. I need to talk with you for a second."

"What's wrong?" he asked.

"That's what I want to talk to you about. Let's go sit in the dugout, and I'll tell you what I know. Deal?"

"Deal," he said.

"I got a call from your grandmother a little while ago. She had to go to Omaha. Seems that your grandfather was having chest pains, so they are going to keep him in the hospital to run some tests."

"How long will he be in the hospital?"

"I'm waiting to hear from Marge. She promised to keep me updated. Anyway, she asked me to look after you for tonight. That okay with you, kid?"

"I guess so. Can we get something to eat? I'm starving."

"Sure, kid. How about some pizza? I know a good place."

"Pizza is great. No anchovies, though. They're yucky."

"I agree, no anchovies. Follow me, my car's right over here."

Chapter - 16

Marge arrived at the hospital and was immediately shown to the cardiac ICU.

The doctor said, "he's had another heart attack, but he refuses any treatment. Maybe you can talk some sense into him."

"I'll try, doctor."

And she walked into her husband's room.

He was hooked up to so many tubes and looked so frail. How could he go downhill so fast, she thought?

"Steve, it's me, Marge."

"I'm so happy to see you, Marge. I have something that needs to be said. Preferably now."

"Not now, Steve. Rest is what you need."

"NO! NOW!" he shouted so loud that the nurse ordered him to calm down or there would be no more visitors.

"Okay, now then," she said.

Struggling for the right words, he finally decided to plow on, "I know I've been a horse's ass for too many years, and for that, I'm sorry. I fell in love with you the first moment I saw you at the Huskers game. I knew then that we would get married. You've been a good wife and deserved better from me." Out of breath now, he struggled to get out one last thought, "Please tell Elaine I was wrong, and I never stopped loving her."

"I will, Steve. I need to talk to the doctor and let him know that your mind is made up. I'll be back in 5 minutes."

"I'm going to rest my eyes now. Give my love to Frankie. I'm going to miss him the most."

"Hush now," Marge said. "You'll be home in no time."

"You may be right, Marge; you may be right. I am heading home."

She knew then that he just gave up and there was no changing his mind. Brave to the end, she thought. I'm going to miss him so much. And the tears flowed as the memories washed over her.

Gladys woke Frankie up early the next morning.

Gently shaking him, she said, "Time to get up, kid. Your grandmother just got back from Omaha."

"Is Grandpa with her?"

"She didn't say. She just asked me to bring you over there."

"Okay. I need to use the bathroom first, though."

"I figured as much. There's a new toothbrush on the counter and some fresh towels for you."

"Thank you, ma'am."

"You can call me Gladys. Everyone else does."

"Okay. Thanks, Gladys."

"No problem, kid. I'll wait for you on the porch. Take your time."

Losing his grandpa just after he got to know him was devastating. His grandma was doing okay, but she looked really sad. His mom was due to arrive any minute now. Everything was happening too fast for Frankie. He just wanted to see his grandpa again. He knew that wasn't possible, though. Just like his father, Grandpa was gone forever.

His mother ran through the door and grabbed her mother in a big hug. Noticing Frankie standing behind his grandma, she motioned for him to join in the hug. Together, they let the tears flow unabated. Each shedding tears for their own separate reasons. Frankie for the loss of yet another person he loves. Marge, for the loss of the man she devoted 35 years to. And Elaine, for the loss of innocence, blames her father.

After the tears subsided, Elaine asked her mother about the plans when she noticed Frankie wearing a Slinky on his arm.

"Where on earth did you get that thing?" she asked while pointing at the Slinky.

"Grandpa gave it to me."

"Really, Grandpa?" She couldn't believe what she was hearing. "Where did he get it?"

"He said he found it in a box out in the shed. Said it was yours and I should ask you why you saved it. Oh, he also wanted me to ask you about this card," he said as he reached into his shirt pocket and pulled out Pernell, "Slinky' Whitiker's card."

She took the card and was at a loss for words for a few seconds, "Where did you find this?"

"In your closet. Grandpa said it was okay to look through your stuff. You're not mad, are you?"

"No, Frankie, I'm not angry. I'm a little confused now, but I'm beginning to figure things out. Here, you keep the card. Someday soon, I'll explain everything. I promise."

"Pinky swear," Frankie said.

"Pinky swear," his mother said, and they hooked pinkies.

The funeral was the next day. It's what grandpa wanted, his mother said. Not many people showed up at the funeral home, and even fewer at the cemetery. There was no church service. Not even a minister to say a few words.

One of Steve's friends who did show up spoke about growing up with him and how they used to raise hell. His stories were funny, but nothing could take away the emptiness Frankie was feeling inside.

Standing beside the open grave, Frankie was trying his best not to cry when he looked up and saw Mr. Whitiker walking toward them.

Confused, Frankie said to his mother, "That's Mr. Whitiker, Mom. He manages the Corn Huskers. Why is he here?"

As Mr. Whitiker reached them, both Elaine and her mother began crying all over again.

"I'm sorry for your loss, Elaine."

"Thank you, Mr. Whitiker," she said and then blew her nose. "It was kind of you to come."

Looking at Frankie's grandma, he said, "I'm so sorry for your loss, Marge. He was a good man."

"Thank you, Pernell. Thank you for coming. We'll be having some people back to the house after we leave here. We'd love to have you drop by to chat about some things."

"Gee, Marge, I got the guys waiting on me at the field right now. I don't think I can make it."

"I understand Pernell. Good to see you again."

"Aw gee Mr. Whitiker. Can't you stop by for a few minutes?" Frankie asked.

"Sorry, kid. We got a big game tomorrow, so I need to work on the basics with the guys."

To Marge and Elaine, he said, "This kid right here is the reason we did so good this season. He made me realize that getting back to the basics was the way to go. Win or lose. Right kid?"

"Yes, sir," he replied.

"Say, kid. Do you happen to have that card on you?"

"I sure do."

Pulling it out of his pocket, he showed it to Mr. Whitiker.

"Still want me to sign it, kid?"

"You bet I do. Here it is."

As he began to sign the card, it occurred to him that he didn't even know the kid's name.

"Say, kid, I'm a little embarrassed, but I never got your name."

"It's Frankie, sir."

"That's a fine name." He signed the card and handed it back to Frankie. "I'll be going now. Again, I'm very sorry for your loss."

He turned and walked away.

Frankie looked down and noticed the card. He turned it over to read what Mr. Whitiker wrote. It said, *'To Frankie, The bestest Grandson ever. Love, Grandpa.'*

"Mom, look at this."

She read the card and nodded. All at once, everything fell into place for Frankie. He ran after Mr. Whitiker, yelling for him to stop. He did stop and turn around.

Frankie ran up to him, gave him a great big hug, and said, "You can't just walk away, Mr. Whit......I mean, Grandpa. I just don't think I want to lose another grandpa just yet."

THE END